"Every pastor needs to read thi vulnerable. If you think you aren't—you're especially at risk. *Don't Blow Up Your Ministry* is grounded in biblical wisdom and practical experience. It's chock-full of real-life applications. If you are a leader in ministry, don't miss out on Michael MacKenzie's life-giving message."
Les and Leslie Parrott, authors of *Saving Your Marriage Before It Starts*

"As 'successful' leaders it's easy for us to become so busy helping others discover who they are 'in Christ' that we forget to apply those truths to ourselves. Mike shares wisdom and discernment that is founded in a both a solid head knowledge and passionate heart knowledge of God's Word honed through decades of in-the-trenches experience in helping those who have spent their lives helping others. He goes beyond describing and defining the problem to detailing practical ways to not just get through but actually learn from and grow through the dark and difficult times in the process of becoming more than conquerors. God has given Mike a comforting, convicting, encouraging, and empowering message that will provide help and hope for anyone who has felt discouraged, defeated, overwhelmed, and ready to give up. This is one of those rich books that you'll want to read more than once."
Gary J. Oliver, executive director of the Center for Healthy Relationships and professor of psychology and practical theology at John Brown University

"Michael MacKenzie knows what brokenness and wholeness in the lives of leaders look like. For years he has dealt with both in their various forms (moral, spiritual, emotional, relational) at the Marble Retreat in Colorado, where leaders come when life is in the process of (as he puts it) blowing up. MacKenzie's book (his first) is a must-read for any man, woman, or married couple in leadership who seek to chart a new path in the direction of lifelong resilience and effectiveness."
Gail and Gordon MacDonald, authors and speakers

"Serving and leading in the local church places pastors and church leaders at a difficult intersection. The pressure to perform coupled with awareness (or denial) of our own sin, brokenness, and fragility leave us dangerously vulnerable to a wide variety of potential pitfalls. In this book, Michael MacKenzie offers us a sobering reality check right alongside immense hope. Out of our shame, fear, and pain, God can still bring about surprising good, and *Don't Blow Up Your Ministry* presents a compelling first word in a critically important ongoing conversation."
Jay Y. Kim, pastor and author of *Analog Church*

"With grace and compassion, Mike MacKenzie poignantly lays out the necessity for pastors to receive their own pastoral care. He invites pastors to dig deep, exploring the underlying issues that if unattended could result not only in personal harm but in communal damage. His intimate knowledge of pastors who've struggled, combined with his clinical expertise, gives weight and heartache to the many people who could've benefited from this book years ago. This is an essential read for every pastor, every ministry worker, and every seminary student. You are loved, you are not alone, and you, too, need care."

Bethany Dearborn Hiser, author of *From Burned Out to Beloved: Soul Care for Wounded Healers* and director of soul care for Northwest Family Life

"This book is not just for pastors but a guide for each of us, from the professionally trained to those who volunteer. Why? Because we all started with a passion, a calling, a felt ministry for those we came alongside. It contributed to our sense of significance, developed compassion, and created feelings of belonging while caring for others. Yet this sense of serving and sacrifice can get us into trouble, wear us out, and make us hate what we used to love! Though *Don't Blow Up Your Ministry* focuses on pastors, the concepts are applicable to all who serve, both in a vocation or as a volunteer. Don't destroy what you love doing most. Be proactive, drawing on the safeguards and practices laid out in *Don't Blow Up Your Ministry*, and looking back you will be grateful for the long-lasting, immense satisfaction of your calling."

Dave Carder, licensed marriage and family therapist, author of *Anatomy of an Affair*

DON'T BLOW UP YOUR MINISTRY

DEFUSE THE UNDERLYING ISSUES THAT TAKE PASTORS DOWN

MICHAEL MᴀᴄKENZIE

An imprint of InterVarsity Press
Downers Grove, Illinois

InterVarsity Press
P.O. Box 1400, Downers Grove, IL 60515-1426
ivpress.com
email@ivpress.com

InterVarsity Press® is the book-publishing division of InterVarsity Christian Fellowship/USA®,
a movement of students and faculty active on campus at hundreds of universities, colleges,
and schools of nursing in the United States of America, and a member movement of
the International Fellowship of Evangelical Students. For information about local
and regional activities, visit intervarsity.org.

All Scripture quotations, unless otherwise indicated, are taken from The Holy Bible,
New International Version®, NIV®. Copyright © 1973, 1978, 1984, 2011 by Biblica, Inc.™
Used by permission of Zondervan. All rights reserved worldwide. www.zondervan.com.
The "NIV" and "New International Version" are trademarks registered in the United States
Patent and Trademark Office by Biblica, Inc.™

While any stories in this book are true, some names and identifying information
may have been changed to protect the privacy of individuals.

Figures designed by Crystal Sutherland, Tüsdé Productions

Cover design and image composite: David Fassett
Interior design: Jeanna Wiggins
Image: old-fashioned explosive: © Tetra Images / Getty Images

ISBN 978-0-8308-4168-4 (print)
ISBN 978-0-8308-4169-1 (digital)

Printed in the United States of America ♾

InterVarsity Press is committed to ecological stewardship and to the conservation of natural
resources in all our operations. This book was printed using sustainably sourced paper.

Library of Congress Cataloging-in-Publication Data
Names: Mackenzie, Michael C., 1969- author.
Title: Don't blow up your ministry : defuse the underlying issues that take
  pastors down / Michael Mackenzie.
Description: Downers Grove, IL : InterVarsity Press, [2021] | Includes
  bibliographical references.
Identifiers: LCCN 2021030780 (print) | LCCN 2021030781 (ebook) | ISBN
  9780830841684 (print) | ISBN 9780830841691 (digital)
Subjects: LCSH: Clergy—Mental health. | Burn out (Psychology)—Religious
  aspects—Christianity. | Clergy—Job stress. | Pastoral theology.
Classification: LCC BV4398 .M33 2021 (print) | LCC BV4398 (ebook) | DDC
  248.8/92—dc23
LC record available at https://lccn.loc.gov/2021030780
LC ebook record available at https://lccn.loc.gov/2021030781

P 25 24 23 22 21 20 19 18 17 16 15 14 13 12 11 10 9 8 7 6 5 4 3 2 1
Y 37 36 35 34 33 32 31 30 29 28 27 26 25 24 23 22 21

THIS BOOK IS DEDICATED TO MY WIFE, KARI.

Your faith, beauty, and love have blessed so many,

but none more than our boys and me. I am very fortunate

to have you as my wife. Thank you for all the sacrifices

you made so this book could be possible.

CONTENTS

FOREWORD

Marshall Shelley

M Y MOTHER ENJOYED GARDENING, and she taught me that weeding was not just about clearing away the visible intruders you could see among the vegetables or flowers. It was what's underground that had to be dealt with.

So my naive efforts to remove the blossoms, leaves, and vines of the dandelions or thistles or Creeping Charlie made things look better for a day or two, but I'd not really accomplished anything. The weeds quickly returned and even spread farther! Unless I had removed the root, I learned, I hadn't done any real weeding.

Mike MacKenzie's decades of work with ministry leaders reveals a similar reality. When a pastor or missionary or parachurch worker is found guilty of adultery or addiction or abusive outbursts, the temptation is to focus on the unacceptable behavior and get it stopped. But cleaning up only what's visible does not solve the problem. The behavior may disappear for a while, but it almost always returns and even spreads further. The problem is the root. And this book helps us recognize the deeper, less visible areas that produce the unacceptable behaviors.

I first became aware of Mike and Kari MacKenzie through Marble Retreat, a center in Colorado that focused on helping ministers and ministry couples in crisis. For many years, Mike was Marble's clinical director, and while I was editor of *Leadership Journal*, he wrote helpful articles for us.

Back in 1979, Marble Retreat founder Louis McBurney had written a book, *Every Pastor Needs a Pastor*, that first introduced me and many others to the underground roots of destructive behavior among ministry leaders. It brought awareness of the deep psychological issues that plague those in ministry and leadership settings. Things such as contentment, insecurity, the need for approval, honesty, internal dialogue, self-worth, and identity.

In the years since Mike and Kari became the leaders of Marble Retreat, their insights and approach have developed further. The hundreds of guests they've worked with in intensive ten-day retreats have revealed additional lessons about spiritual and psychological health that are necessary for those in stressful leadership roles.

Don't Blow Up Your Ministry: Defuse the Underlying Issues That Take Pastors Down shares those lessons through the stories of many of the leaders who sought and found help with Mike and Kari MacKenzie. You will learn to not be content with surface treatments of destructive behavior. You will develop the ability to look beneath the surface to address the root causes. I enthusiastically commend this book to you.

INTRODUCTION

The Powers and the Dangers in the Lives of Pastors

B EING A CHRISTIAN LEADER is a dangerous job.

I grew up in Prince Edward Island, Canada, the son of a lobster fisherman. The TV shows *Wicked Tuna* and *Deadliest Catch* show how deadly commercial fishing is. Men can lose their limbs or even their lives from the dangers of working at sea.

One day when I was fishing with my father we were running off a set of lobster traps. Fishermen tie six traps together, weight them to sink to the bottom, and attach a buoy on each end. The traps line the edge of the boat and the captain steers to where he believes the best catch is. Then the crew sets the traps by pushing the first one over into the sea. The first one drags the next one overboard and one by one they drag the entire set of traps into the sea.

My father gave the nod to drop a set of traps and I pushed the first one overboard. We reached the last trap when he suddenly slammed the boat into reverse, almost knocking me off balance. I looked toward the cabin with an expression of, "What the heck?" My annoyance turned to gratitude when my father pointed to the rope wrapped around my foot about to pull me overboard.

3

Multiple men on P.E.I. (Prince Edward Island) have lost their lives fishing, including one of my best friends. What makes it so dangerous? Some of the factors include the dangerous equipment; the ever-changing movement of the sea and corresponding instability on deck; working through storms with their powerful waves; and the weariness caused by the long hours of heavy work. An additional risk at play was making the same fatal mistake many make—going out to sea alone.

Many get caught in nets or rope and have been dragged overboard into the sea. They don't always end up losing their lives; some only suffer injuries. Why did they survive? Because someone was there to pull them out. And countless others are spared injury because someone was there to warn them of trouble. Being a Christian leader is a dangerous job. If someone tries to go it alone, to not seek help, damage and even destruction can result.

Power saves. Power in the hands of Churchill saved many lives. Power destroys. Power in the hands of Hitler destroyed lands and cities and huge numbers of people.

There is power in the position of the Christian leader. If we have influence, we have power, we have capacity, we have potential. This power is carried in a container, a vessel. In this case, the vessel is the Christian leader. The vessel is under pressure. Pressure without, power within. If the vessel is not cared for and the pressure is too much, the result is ignition and explosion.

Collateral damage is unintended damage, injuries, or death due to an action. The last thing a Christian leader thinks he will do is harm the church, the kingdom, or bring shame to the name of Christ. Yet because many Christian leaders underestimate the power they have and the pressure they are under, they end up destroying their own lives and ministries and hurting others around them.

4

TIME BOMB

Pastor Josh is a gifted leader. God gave him the gifts of wisdom, vision, and compassion, perhaps the gifting trifecta for ministry leaders. People were drawn to him and most felt like he ministered to them with great doses of grace and truth.

The problem was that Josh was becoming hollow inside. For many years Josh had this vague sense of shame. In his twenties and thirties, he would power through it by performance. If he sensed feelings of inadequacy or caught himself rehearsing negative messages, then he would take that anxious energy and refocus it on doing better. It seemed to be a great system for which he received a lot of outside affirmation, but no one knew what was fueling his drive on the inside. Everyone made the assumption that his drivenness was Spirit led, not realizing much of it was the product of shame. Josh not only let people think this but actively presented it as his cover.

Several situations came together to set up the perfect storm for Josh's shipwreck. First, the church he was leading began to grow quickly and Josh was taking on more and more administrative and managerial roles. He struggled to delegate well and was becoming critical of staff—wanting them to do things like he would do things. Second, Josh's teenage daughter was rebelling. Not rebelling in some little way but in every way. Being the pastor of a conservative church in a medium-sized town made this embarrassing for him. Third, his marriage to Kate was growing increasingly cold and tense. Her voice said it had to do with the amount of time he spent in ministry and the lack of time with her. But those words were a distant echo compared to the sirens of shoulds pounding in his ears from the pressing needs of ministry.

Josh poured more and more into his ministry but was feeling more and more depleted and numb. He became increasingly irritated with people and found himself stewing and chewing on the slightest of criticisms perceived or otherwise. He initially began filling his evening schedule with meetings in order to keep up with the growing demands of the church, but he partially did it to avoid going home. When he was at home it seemed like every conversation turned into an argument with his wife or kids. And while he didn't want to, he would end up lecturing them and then withdrawing.

Josh didn't know who he was anymore. This once compassionate, patient, and wise pastor, father, and husband was quickly becoming rude, impatient, and distant from everyone who mattered to him.

After a particularly difficult meeting regarding the building project where he accepted the lead role in raising $1.5 million in six months, he returned to his office feeling overwhelmed and angry. Before he knew it, he was visiting a porn site. *What in the world am I doing?* he thought. He had not had a problem with porn use in fourteen years.

He also noticed that he was drinking more. While his theology and church context had always allowed for a social drink now and then, he noticed he was always ordering an alcoholic beverage with lunch and dinner. Josh was spiraling out of control and was very close to losing his wife and ministry. Josh was living by a doomsday clock and it read two minutes to midnight. Without an intervention, his world was going to implode.

WHY DOES A PASTOR NEED HELP?

A pastor is limited like everyone else: limited in gifting, in energy, limited in self-knowledge even. Wendell Berry, an astute observer of the human condition, particularly of the Christian leader, writes, "The task of healing is to respect oneself as a creature, no more and no less."[1] Being limited, one of the needs we have is for someone in our life who speaks God's words to us, someone to whom we can confess, someone we've given authority to speak to our blind spots or to our outright rebellion. Someone we can turn to when we are confused, overwhelmed, tempted, tired, or full of grief. A pastor is like anyone else trying to make it through this life—they need help. Pastors play an important and much needed role in people's lives yet often negate having someone play the same role in their life.

Pastor Josh's power and influence were ramping up. Sadly, and correspondingly, the vessel holding this power was breaking down under the pressure. Josh was about to implode and then explode. Lots and lots of collateral damage. Could the explosion be avoided? Yes, and even better, the exact same ingredients creating the bomb could be used for deep healing and growth in Josh.

My wife, Kari, and I are the directors and therapists at Marble Retreat, a counseling center for Christian leaders. We have spent the past twenty years specializing in caring for those who work full time professionally for the kingdom. We've done this because we believe in the importance of roles like those of pastor, missionary, worship leader, or family pastor. We do this work because we know ministry is a hard road and it wears on those who do it and they need someone to care for them. We do this because we care about and admire those who are willing to wholeheartedly serve the Lord—these people of the Word.

We grew a heart to care for these folks out of experience as well. Kari was on the mission field in China for three years and saw the need for missionaries and missionary teams to have someone they could turn to for help, encouragement, and direction. And when an influential pastor in her life fell morally, she went to talk with him to try and understand what happened. In his story she heard how the church was not there for him when he needed someone—before and after his fall.

One of my closest friends when I was growing up was the son of my pastor, who was my spiritual father in many ways. My pastor died of a heart attack at age fifty-two. Being in their home and life I saw many of the challenges of ministry and how it can affect your life and family. And my older brother went into church planting. His experience again showed me the many different potential trials of being in full-time ministry.

This book comes from the desire to spare Christian leaders, their families, and the church the loss, destruction, and grief that come when a shepherd explodes. Too often we sit with leaders who with gut wrenching sobs lament the damage that has been done. Too often we hear the words, "I wish I would have known about or worked on these issues ten years ago."

But this book is about hope for the Christian leader. Hope that disaster can be averted and from within the struggles can come deeper meaning, peace, faith, and love. Hope that what you preach and teach others is also true for you: that God is for you and he can heal you and set you free.

PART ONE

DANGEROUS OCCUPATION

HOW ONE PASTOR BLEW UP

W HEN WE HAVE QUESTIONS about God who do we look to? The pastor. That is a lot of pressure on one individual.

With pressures like that, it is easy to see how an explosion can occur.

But out in the world there are even more dangers for the pastor than those questions. Here is one account of a pastor who did not take stock of the dangers facing him and the stress that would eventually take its toll. By looking specifically at one instance we can see how quietly and secretly these dangers can slip into our lives, like a person infiltrating with a bomb to be set off later.

Pastor Craig came to a Marble Retreat. He had been caught having an affair with a woman in his church.

This event would not seem to depict the man who grew up as an average kid in Ohio. His was a nice family, but he might use a different word than *average*. He had very perfectionistic expectations in his home.

"I wasn't able to meet up to Mom and Dad's feelings about my school performance and my attempts to be an athlete," he said. "I regularly fell flat on my face compared to Dan, my brother. He scored high on all his tests and made great grades, and he lettered four years in basketball and football.

"My average abilities were not enough. So my motto became, 'Work harder to make up for my lack of natural gifts.' With hard work I used what God had given me and stretched myself as far as I could."

Craig was creative. He was intelligent. He was articulate. He was passionate about God using him to do great things. And God did.

Pastor Craig was in a ministry for many years as an associate pastor. And then he got a call to go to a church that had leveled off over its last several years at about two hundred people. They asked Pastor Craig to come and lead the church. The community was growing and there was a lot of opportunity for the church if they could get moving in the right direction.

Craig is full of vision, ideas, and passion. He is a cheerleader. He is an equipper who can get older people on the move and excited. So he went. Things began to happen. God began to work and expand his ministry.

But Craig told us something wasn't right; life was off a little to one side.

"I still felt insecure and inadequate. I felt like an impostor; a cover up was going on in my life."

What did he use to cover up his insecurities? More plodding on the path of work and climbing the hill of accomplishment.

"I felt I could basically fool people into believing that I was a more intelligent, more faithful man than I really was if I hid behind this curtain of work," Pastor Craig said. "If people really got to know me well, I sincerely felt the show would be over . . ."

Reality seemed to confirm Craig's strategy. The church began to take off and went from 200 to 300 to 400 to 500 people. They went through a couple of building campaigns that resulted in a new multimillion-dollar facility that would seat 2,000 people.

Craig was grateful for his success. Still the feelings of inadequacy and insecurity grew. So did the expectations that every Sunday he would take a big swing from the pulpit and knock it out of the park. Which he did. Naturally people expected more and more. The board members and congregation wanted a new and bigger vision for the expanding ministry as it grew. Craig attacked the challenges the only way he knew how.

"I ended up working longer hours. I stole time and energy from myself and from my wife and family. I depleted myself emotionally and spiritually . . . then she came along."

Samantha, a young, attractive woman with her own problems, came to Pastor Craig for counseling. Her marriage was falling apart. Samantha began to sympathize with Craig's unbelievable burdens of ministry and the challenges he had with the overall growth and certain individuals who regularly challenged him. She empathized and it felt good to him. Someone finally understood the sacrifices he was making for the church and for members like her. Hardworking Craig could have heard some of the same sympathy from his wife; but he was too busy.

Craig began to break his own boundaries about meeting with a woman alone. He met with Samantha behind closed doors for coffee. The conversation began to slide into personal conversations of frustration with marriage and with family, and of course with the church. She grew in her care and compassion for him and eventually it led to the slippery slope of a sexual affair.

The church leadership found out about the affair when she confessed it to Craig's wife and the elders. Then the damage started happening. The church terminated him. The church started struggling without a leader. His marriage was hanging by a thread. And Pastor Craig came to a Marble Retreat for counseling as do many pastors with feelings of despair and self-hatred.

The big question in his mind loomed. "Why, why did I do this? I had my dream job and everything was going great. God was blessing everything I touched. And why would I blow this up now? Why would I blow up this ministry and my life when I had finally arrived at where I wanted to be as a church leader, a pastor, and a man? Wasn't a large and successful ministry what I'd always wanted?"

When you are sitting with someone, even a ministry leader, who has made some very bad choices and is reaping the fallout you see the human tendency to blame surface issues such as "I was tired and working too much" or "my wife and I were not connecting anymore." You also see the human tendency to want to just clean up the mess and go back to doing it the same way. Seeing this tendency can be very convicting as I can see how I do the exact same thing in my own life. As a Christian therapist I believe and see how God desires to do so much more in us. Heart change. Soul healing. This gives us a completely different vantage point from which to do life and ministry. So we go beneath the surface to the rest of the iceberg.

Craig did not realize how underlying issues had affected his choices. They kept him from facing his problems head on. Perfectionism and insecurity drove him to prove to others he could do what he set his mind to. He believed that his willingness to work harder than everyone else would gain affirmation from others and especially from women.

He added one fallacious statement after another: "If I get good enough I'll keep growing the church and that will keep everyone happy." "Raise the budget and then everything will be okay."

CHALLENGES IN THE PASTORATE

While numerous pastors stay healthy and serve faithfully, many are hurting. Barna's state of pastors report in 2017 found some of the areas in which pastors struggle:

- More than one-third of pastors are at high or medium risk of burnout, and three-quarters know at least one fellow pastor whose ministry ended due to stress.

- Forty-three percent of pastors are at high or medium relational risk, whether they are experiencing challenges in marriage, family, friendships or other close relationships.

- One in five pastors has struggled with an addiction—most commonly to porn.

- Almost half of pastors have faced depression.[1]

When a pastor leaves ministry because they have fallen morally or burned out there is a huge ripple effect on the congregation and community they were serving.

GOING DEEPER

Craig came to Marble and we began to dig around in what was going on underneath, because he knew it wasn't just lust that got him into this. The affair was just an indicator of why it happened.

We talked about the need for affirmation, compassion, empathy, and feelings of concern that drew him into the affair. Samantha convinced him he was not alone when they were together. But he searched for affirmation in the wrong place. And her confession to the elders sealed that wrong choice.

Craig needs a sense of adequacy and security first and foremost in Christ. He needed to let God touch and heal the shame he had been carrying his whole life. He needed intimacy with his wife, which had been missing for many years. He needed to get off the treadmill of proving himself and be free to be who he was and walk in *his* calling. God had gifted him in many ways. He did not have to prove that to anybody.

These were some of the things Craig came to realize were driving his affair. But at this point he had caused a lot of damage. Sadly so. During one of the group sessions or "intensives," as we call them, he said, "I just wish I had come here ten years ago. I wish I had realized these things. I wish I had taken precautions and dealt with what was in my own heart and in my own home. And maybe I would not have gone down this road."

Pastor Craig felt great grief and shame about the disgrace he had brought to God's name and the church's name.

But there was redemption. There was forgiveness and there was grace for him. And we'll find those responses in the stories of this book.

REFLECTION QUESTIONS

1. Do you relate to Craig in some way?
2. Are there some behaviors in your life or way of doing ministry that you are concerned about?
3. Do you see your own personal or family of origin issues trailing along with you?
4. Can you connect the dots of how your own brokenness could lead to blowing up your life and ministry?
5. If you are not getting help with your struggles, what is keeping you from doing so?

2

GOING IT ALONE

L INDA FOUNDED AND WORKED at a large Christian relief organization in Africa. She had grown up in a highly toxic
home where she unfortunately had experienced sexual abuse.
Partly due to the pain she carried and partly due to the influence
of her friends she started using drugs. Soft drugs at first and
then progressively more hard drugs, including cocaine. By the
time she reached young adulthood she needed a way to finance
her habit so she went into prostitution.

As happens so often when God is at work, she found herself at
the end of herself and to her own amazement wound up in a local
church one Sunday morning. The message was too good to be
true—a Father who loved her, a Savior who saved her, and healing
from sin and shame. She grabbed hold of this truth and walked
away from her life determined to follow God.

A problem Linda had left over from her previous life was that
she had an issue with men and that is what brought her to Marble
Retreat. She had conflict with her ministry team, especially the
men. She wound up in a group with several male pastors and
when she told her life story they wept with her and for her. I was

her individual therapist and I soon realized the antagonistic position she wished to put me in. She tried to draw me into conflict by challenging or undermining suggestions or feedback I gave. She tried to get me to condemn or shame her with leading statements such as, "But I deserve to be alone, rejected, or to fail, don't I?"

It can be challenging to care for someone who is purposefully trying to antagonize you and draw you into conflict. Especially when your temperament tends to be conflict avoidant like mine. One of my hockey-playing construction-working buddies said to me, "It must be nice to get paid to talk for a living." I responded, "I get paid to listen, and it is not as easy as you would think."

In situations like these I try and remember several truths. First, don't get caught up in the immediate; don't take the bait for conflict. See the pattern and how it is revealing something about this person's pain. Second, I pray God will help me see them as he does. And third, I remember some of the most healing moments of my life have been when the ugliness of my own heart is on display, yet someone receives me with love, acceptance, and compassion, instead of reaction.

After initially either tolerating or ignoring the men in the group, Linda began to grow in her irritation and then animosity toward them. In the name of helping them grow she began to pounce on any little infraction she saw a man commit, cutting them down with evil-eyed looks and acidic words. She did not have any grace on the wives either, communicating they were weak in not being harder on their husbands.

Linda was hardest on herself and while the group was trying to love her, she struggled to receive it.

AT RISK AND ALONE

We have seen pastors for burnout, affairs, anxiety, depression, spiritual crisis, termination of their position, grief, recovery from cancer, trauma, and many more of life's rabbit punches. If the Christian leader would have had someone who was deeply ministering to them how would it have played out differently? Would they even find themselves in burnout or an affair? Would their recovery be a normal outcome of life in the body of Christ?

Even when they have hit bottom, the pathway out is to have someone who ministers to them. Wendell Berry writes, "Healing is impossible in loneliness; it is the opposite of loneliness. Conviviality is healing."[1]

The number one contributing factor creating issues for those in ministry is isolation.[2]

Ben shared in group how he knew he was burning out and was in trouble emotionally and in danger of crossing some lines in his exhausted state. He mustered the courage to tell his elders of his dilemma. One influential board member who was the CEO of a large corporation responded harshly with, "You have no idea of what real pressure is, what it is like in the real world." The other elders responded with silence. Pastor Ben pulled it back together and got on with the business of the meeting. A few months later Ben did burnout and fall morally.

Many of those sitting in the pews still do not understand how difficult the role is for their pastor. The not funny "Must be nice to only work one hour a week" comments based on frustrations regarding a pastor setting boundaries around their free time shows how others perceive the position. And of course, pastors cannot get up front on a Sunday morning and lament the challenges of their roles. It takes leadership accepting that the pastor's role is difficult, planning to support the pastor, and educating the church on the difficulty of the role and how as a church they will support their pastor.

Lifeway Research found, "Almost half of those who left the pastorate said their church wasn't doing any of the kinds of things that would help." Ed Stetzer, executive director of Wheaton College's Billy Graham Center, adds, "Having clear documents, offering a sabbatical rest, and having people help with weighty counseling cases are key things experts tell us ought to be in place."[3] Churches could do a few of these simple strategic interventions to help the well-being of the pastor.

Another pastor, Sheldon, painfully shared his story of how he went to the leadership because he was at the end of his rope. The feelings of pain, fear, and sadness overwhelmed him in the meeting because he had finally opened the door on how he was feeling. This left him sobbing uncontrollably. The immediate assessment of the leadership was that Sheldon was emotionally and mentally unstable and not capable of performing his duties when in reality he needed to grieve, be understood, and be supported. Unfortunately, through their response the church's leadership pushed the knife in a little deeper by showing Sheldon that his fears were real—that no one understood or cared about his pain and would judge him for being "broken" if he shared how he felt.

Churches, mission organizations, and other organizations in which Christian leaders serve are not always the ones to blame for a pastor experiencing lack of support. Quite often, the pastors themselves are to blame. Many Christian leaders desire to serve, not be served. They are willing to sacrifice for the greater good. They minimize their own needs and desire to walk by faith, which can get defined as walking alone. While a leader can biblically back this approach, one thing is lacking: the biblical and wise reality of pastors needing the community to support and sacrifice for them as well.

We were working with a young, talented, passionate ministry couple who were leading a church plant in a poor and violent community. They were doing incredible ministry, but they were undersupported, underresourced, and were quickly burning out. When we suggested they ask the ministry leadership for what they needed they quickly responded that they could never do that. When we had them unpack why, it came down to two major issues for them: they did not want to admit they "couldn't make it work," and it felt selfish to them. After some reinforcement from the therapy group of how they would completely burn out if they didn't ask for help, this young couple had a meeting at the ministry headquarters. Much to their surprise and pleasure, the leadership was more than happy to work at better meeting their needs. But many in ministry never ask. It is important for those in ministry to understand the internal factors that contribute to why they don't ask for help.

The authors of *Resilient Ministry* found that, "Ministry leaders collapse under the overwhelming pressures to ignore their own needs motivated by busyness, people pleasing, the tyranny of the urgent and their own lack of priority on personal growth."[4] So, while the real and tremendous pressure is true for many in ministry, this pressure often plays right into issues the pastor already struggles with including people pleasing and self-negation.

AN ISOLATING POSITION

Chapters 18 and 19 of 1 Kings record the experience of Elijah and how after the powerful encounter with the prophets of Baal God answered his prayer. Surprisingly after God revealed his power by sending down fire to burn the offering and altar, Elijah fled in fear and isolated himself. He quickly came to believe he was all alone.

Most pastors know they need relationship. They know they need a place to be open about their struggles, but they are also painfully aware voicing their struggles to the wrong person could cost them their jobs. Michael was counseling with a pastor in a private practice and the pastor would begin every session with the question, "You are required by law not to share any of what I am talking about right?" He was not even talking about any deep dark sin or walking on the wrong side of the law. He was talking about his struggles with staff and how to deal with a couple of difficult families in the church. His concern about confidentiality came because he believed if his "negative" thoughts and feelings were known he could lose his job. He was probably right.

Christian leaders often have their sin or weakness painfully exposed. Caught in an affair, using pornography, having an angry outburst in a staff meeting, frustration leaking into a sermon, panic attack on a Sunday morning, or hitting the end of their rope. Soon they come tearfully before leadership saying, "I cannot do it all anymore." All too often the response of the church or leadership in the church is not one of care, redemption, and wisdom but the response is one coming out of their own hurt, judgmentalism, and self-protection.

It is necessary and true that if a pastor crosses certain lines they do need to step down at least for a time. In some cases, the tough decision of their being unable to attend worship services for a time is also necessary but this does not mean that the church cannot still be supportive. We have seen many churches go to great lengths to distance themselves from the "fallen" pastor, even to the point of ostracizing the pastor, spouse, and their family. They are told not to contact anyone at the church.

The grief of the church not being there for them is often the deepest one that pastors are carrying. As one pastor who was caught falling into pornography use said, "I spent twenty years building a church that focused on grace. We poured out grace and acceptance and walked with anyone who was stuck in sin, including sexual brokenness to bring them back into God's will, but when I fell, I was given a check and shown the door and told not to come to church or have my family come because that would be awkward for everyone. And to top it all off it has been several weeks now and we have not heard from anyone! We thought these people were our family and it has been so hurtful to have them turn their backs on us when we needed them most."

A church can help support a pastor in a thousand little ways. The one big way that would most likely contribute to a pastor not leaving ministry is to be there for them when they are hurting and broken. This means continuing in relationship with them. Having conversations with them, caring about their practical needs, finding ways the church can still minister to their family, and in general, continuing to show the pastor they care.

It can be messy and complicated when a pastor breaks, falls, or just plain needs help. A church getting outside help involved can be beneficial. The pastor and their family need the church's support but may need someone from outside the church to be their pastor.

When pastors go it alone it leaves them very vulnerable. The explosive material is under pressure and no one is there to put the fuse out.

DON'T DO IT ALONE

Henri Nouwen writes, "Pain suffered alone feels very different from pain suffered alongside another. Even when the pain stays, we know how great the difference if another draws close, if another shares with us in it. This kind of comfort comes most fully and powerfully visible in the Incarnation, wherein God comes into our midst—into our lives—to remind us, 'I am with you at all times and in all places.'"[5]

We ask the Christian leaders we work with, "When was the last time that you experienced feeling loved?" Often, their response will be an occasion when they exhibited something positive and were rewarded for it. The natural follow up question is, "When have you experienced being loved in your brokenness?" Crickets. Whose fault is this, the pastors' or those around them? Often both.

Many of those in Christian leadership dread dependency because their experience in life has been that no one shows up when they have a need. They make sure they show up for others yet deep down they still fear being vulnerable and risking no one showing up for them.

EVERYONE NEEDS HELP

We have limits, we have needs, we have brokenness, and so we all need help. This includes pastors. Not only is it important to recognize the need, but to fill in that hole in the pastor's life with the support and help which comes from outside the pulpit.

In the opening of her book *Emotionally Focused Couple Therapy with Trauma Survivors*, Susan M. Johnson begins painting a picture about the need and power of relationships:

> If another stands beside you when you face overwhelming terror and helplessness—whether you name this terror and helplessness a "dragon" or call it by some other name, such as traumatic stress—then everything is different. Shadows are not so terrifying. The struggle can be shared, and sometimes

the fight can even be a thing of joy as, together, you defy the dragon. We all know it is better not to be alone in the dark and that connection with others makes us stronger.[6]

Pastors face many dragons, and unfortunately battles are being lost to these dragons. Have pastors tapped into the resource of relationships to face the battles? Has anyone stepped up to stand beside the pastor as they face the dragons by providing care, counsel, and encouragement? Do those within the church who have realized they need someone to help them face the challenges of life realize the pastor needs the same? Pastors need to receive what they give to others—they need to be ministered to during difficult times but also before difficult times. They need someone to pray with and for them, someone to hold up their arms when they cannot, someone to be their friend.

Pastors often do not receive being poured into. Sometimes it is the pastor's resistance. Sometimes it is the negligence of those in relationship with the pastor, and sometimes it is the nature of the beast of ministry. But whatever the cause the truth remains— pastors are people in need of someone to minister to them.

A pastor is human like everyone else, limited in gifting, in energy, in self-knowledge. Part of respecting ourselves as a creature or a person is respecting that we are limited and have needs. We need someone who can help us see the issues beneath the issues. Someone who can help us defuse before we blow.

LINDA—THE REST OF THE STORY

In her individual sessions I continued to show her grace and after building some street cred pointed out to Linda how she was hard on herself and how she was only comfortable with one kind of human interaction—conflict. She had an "aha" moment and could then quickly see how she had been setting up confrontations with men so she could then not only have an excuse to be angry with them but more importantly had an excuse to not get too close, and was protecting herself from receiving any gifts other might have to give her. She needed to forgive the men in her life who had truly hurt her and forgive herself and begin to engage with those others, especially in the body of Christ, with love, truth, and grace.

Now that Linda's pattern was exposed and the shame and lies that fueled it, we could deal directly with it in the group. When someone in the group grieved for her pain instead of letting her ignore it or let it bounce off, we had her sit with it for a while. "What does it mean to you, Linda, that this man is moved to tears because of your pain?" When someone would affirm Linda about her intelligence, faith, or courage instead of letting her use her "whatever" word or attitude, we had her focus on what it felt like to be affirmed.

As Linda's heart began to soften and her walls came down she opened up more to being loved. One day as Linda was wrestling with her feelings of shame my wife and co-therapist, Kari, firmly and gently told Linda to look her in the eyes and listen to her words. "Linda, you are beautiful. You are God's beloved child, made in his image. You are not a prostitute. You are not a drug addict. You are not dirty or less than in any way. You are an amazing woman of God." Linda began to smile and cry, and cry and smile. Healing tears.

The message of God's love and grace Linda heard back in the church that day she wandered in was so sweet and true. Yet, one thing was lacking. She had never experienced it. At least not from herself or from others. She made sure she kept others at arm's length and even set up relationships even within the church to confirm the old shame message that she was bad. In God's love and wisdom, He gave us the body where we could experience the reality of love and grace and forgiveness.

Linda tried to go it alone. In doing so she was not only missing out on real loving relationships, she was missing out on deep healing for herself, and of really experiencing the Father's love.

Don't stay in isolation. It is dangerous.

REFLECTION QUESTIONS

1. Have deep personal relationships fallen down your priority list?
2. Do you have relationships outside of ministry?
3. Do you have someone in your life that you can talk to, really talk to? Talk to about your ministry struggles? Talk to about your personal struggles?
4. Do you need to reconnect with someone who once was this type of friend?
5. Do you need a different kind of community than what you currently have? A support group? A counselor? A coach? A mentor?
6. Do you play a role in your loneliness? If so, what? And how could you do something different?

SHOT BY THE SILVER BULLET

FIRE, READY, AIM

Charlie was a very driven pastor. Like a professional athlete not missing a game he talks of how when his mom died he not only performed her service but he also did not miss preaching at church the following Sunday. He had served at four different churches and he did not take a break between finishing at one and starting at the next. One Sunday he would be preaching his exit sermon and the next Sunday he would be starting fresh at a new church.

When asked why he did ministry this way Charlie was aware of his good motives: "I always want to be giving 100 percent to God, I do not want to waste a minute when there is so much to be done, I just love ministering to others and preaching God's Word." He also had some awareness of the wrong reasons for his drivenness: he liked the praise; he liked being thought of as strong; he was proud of what he did. Charlie would pray and repent when he recognized moments of pride. He would also do a little pastor rationalization—God's work is getting done.

What he did not do was sit with and dig into why he did ministry the way he did. Why did he feel guilty taking a Sunday off? He compulsively needed to always do more ministry. Why did rest seem selfish? He regularly broke the commandment of keeping the Sabbath and wore it like a faith and service badge.

We will see where this got Charlie at the end of this chapter.

WHAT A PASTOR THINKS THEY NEED

Kari and I led a denominational conference for pastors on experiencing God's love. There were many nods and tears from those in attendance but we could also tell some were not into it. I sat at a table with a group of five pastors at a lunch break. When I approached their table, I noticed their conversation abruptly stopped but I did not take the hint and sat down anyway. After a few moments of awkward silence, the outspoken one asked me if they could tell me what they were talking about. "Sure," I said tentatively.

He said, "Well, your topic is fine but what we would really like from our denominational conference is something practical. We were just discussing how it would be more helpful to learn how to break the two hundred in attendance barrier, or have the most effective youth group materials . . ." The rest of his comrades began rapid firing other practical situations with which they desperately wanted help.

It was like they were starving and desperately needing a steak, even a bone to chew on. What these pastors were potentially missing was this: they were stressed, overwhelmed, and doubting their own ability to get the job done well and when feeling this way their first inclination was to get more tools and more information so they could be successful.

Ongoing education and tools are necessary and a good thing, but if not careful pastors take a very dangerous step in ministry by trying to find confidence, security, and peace in one's own abilities and performance.

The president of this denomination had asked us to speak on the topic of God's love and acceptance and providence as he was seeing pastors wearing themselves out trying to do it all. Instead of performance, he wanted them to rest in knowing him and trusting him better.

DOUBLE SHOT

Zach and Tom were in the same group at Marble Retreat. At first glance they could not appear to be any more different. Zach was a slim, good-looking guy, the son of a super pastor. His dad had a large church, a TV ministry, and he had written a dozen books. Zach was groomed from the beginning to walk in his father's footsteps. The dad trained Zach for succession, having those who worked for him give Zach the skills and experience he needed to perform well. After several years of rebellion in young adulthood Zach came back to the faith and the calling on his life and began ministry with guns blazing. His first full-time ministry was as the senior pastor of a five thousand–member, well-respected church. From outside appearance Zach was a natural and in many people's minds he was superior to his father as a dynamic preacher and leader.

Tom, on the other hand, did not grow up in a Christian family. Tom grew up as an "outsider," knowing little about the Christian faith, and even less about how a church works or what a pastor is supposed to do and be. Tom recalls walking past churches in his neighborhood when he was growing up and thinking what a strange mystery it was that was going on in those places.

Tom was into partying and sex in college and was not thinking much about anything else until he got a girl pregnant. She decided to have an abortion and for some reason this bothered Tom. This event and some other troubling times began a soul-searching season for him, and during this time he was invited to a campus ministry. While not an immediate lightning bolt conversion, his relationship with God and commitment to his newfound faith grew. He met a Christian girl, they fell in love, and together they began dreaming of being in ministry. After college Tom went to seminary, and he and his wife excitedly accepted the call to a small church of seventy-five people in Iowa after graduation.

Zach and Tom were both at Marble Retreat for burnout. When Zach unpacked why he was burned out it had to do with a deep sense of personal insecurity, the pressure he felt to perform to keep the church growing, and all the hoops he was having to jump through to keep it all going. Tom spoke of a deep sense of personal insecurity, the pressure he felt to perform and grow his seventy-five-member church. He had hoops at both ends of the court and he was trying to sink every shot.

What were the ways Zach and Tom tried to deal with their own sense of impending burnout before getting help? First, they both kept their mouths shut. They were embarrassed and interpreted their own feelings of inadequacy as being a lack of faith. Zach compared himself to his father who in his mind was never rattled by the expectations but relished them. Tom was comparing himself to pastors out there who obviously did not struggle as he did. This keeping their mouths shut included keeping up a poker face, telling everyone everything was great, and not leaning on anyone else for help or support.

Second, Zach and Tom took the approach of trying harder. More hours at work, more trainings, more programs to try and get it together. "If I can just get to the point where this comes naturally then I can relax." "If I can grow the church to 7,000 then the pressure will be off." "If I grow the church to 125 then the pressure will be off." "If I am better equipped and can produce, then everything will be okay."

Third, they both began dealing with feelings of fear and self-doubt and the stress and pressure through medicating. Zach used sex, beginning with pornography, which escalated into sex with women. Tom returned to the alcohol abuse of his youth.

Zach and Tom got caught in the vicious shame cycle. They would act out, feel incredible shame, make a vow to try harder. Trying harder meant efforts to stop the acting out but also meant giving more to ministry. They would feel the pressure and expectations of ministry juxtaposed against their own feelings of insecurity, and then they would act out again to feel better and numb the pain and it would start all over again. Ironically, many pastors caught in the shame cycle appear to be doing better at ministry because of their increased commitment to do more.

They both were shot by the silver bullet of ministry performance. The silver bullet for many in Christian leadership is being successful in ministry. The silver bullet is supposed to kill any feelings of self-doubt and inadequacy and at the same time provide a sense of adequacy and security and competence. The most common path to getting the silver bullet is to work harder.

But ministry performance does not fix underlying issues. It is a distraction at best and keeps them from dealing with their deeper brokenness, and at worst adds fuel to the fire on the path to burnout.

THE BULLET

There are several dangers when trying to catch the silver bullet:

- Working harder will end in burnout, as will trying to hold on to "success."
- Ministry and ministry success become about me, what I can do.
- Being successful will not scratch the itch as it is really a soul problem.

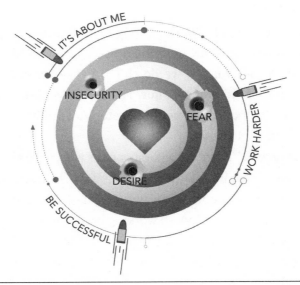

Figure 3.1. Silver bullet misses the heart

Pastors work harder and put more pressure on themselves to address their heart issues, but this approach misses the heart and can lead to increased fear and insecurity.

Why is going after the silver bullet such a trap? I asked a couple of recovering workaholic Christian leaders their opinion. Merle is head of a church planting and leadership training ministry. He works with a lot of pastors. Here are some of his thoughts on why pastors turn to workaholism:

We are fragile. "From what I've been able to gather, many of the pastors who I have connected with are 'fragile' people, myself included. I say 'fragile' because we don't have the strength and depth, from a spiritual formation perspective and an identity in Christ perspective, to consistently withstand the unbiblical expectations of our congregations, the ongoing assaults of our flesh, and the shrewd deceptions of the demonic."

We are egotistical. "Working long and hard is a badge that some of us wear to show how committed we are to 'the Lord's work,' when in actuality, we do this because we get a lot of stroking from it. Before you know it, we have walked ourselves right into a 'works-based' reward system/mentality that fuels our flesh but kills our soul."

We are afraid. "There are a number of us who, if we are honest, would have to admit that our workaholism is driven in some ways by our fears. We may fear vocational obsolescence (especially those of us over fifty), so working harder/longer gives us a false sense of security. We may fear failure, so we work harder/longer to try to control as much as we can to give us a false sense of controlling the outcomes."

We are adrenaline junkies. "There is a sense in which, for some of us, working harder/longer fuels our insatiable need to be 'on,' and 'on' at a high-level of activity and intensity. We have to be constantly stimulated by problems that need to be solved, innovations that we want to be at the forefront of, massive events that will showcase our talents/workaholism, and crises that only we can resolve (or so we think)."[1]

Steve, the founder and president of an international ministry and an author, had this to say about the danger of workaholism in the ministry:

"For me it was the sense that time off was selfish. I grew up in a household where "being productive" was emphasized. The TV was never allowed to be on during the day. If you were unoccupied, you needed to be given work to do. 'Idle hands are the devil's workshop,' that sort of thing. It is easy to believe in a grace-oriented salvation while living a works-based life.

"People feel free to critique your life, often to your face. 'Our last pastor . . .' Some years ago, my car was in the shop and a friend loaned us her spiffy sports car convertible. I got more smart remarks about that than I can count. 'Looks like we are paying you too much!' came one passive-aggressive remark cloaked in humor. The consequence is that we feel that we are constantly trying to please our critics. 'Look at what his wife is wearing today . . .'

"You feel it is your duty to help everyone. I could never feel good about taking a vacation when I knew I had brothers and sisters in Christ being persecuted for their faith. You recall the story of Jesus seeking rest and the people coming to him and he let them. That's the model.

"The life of a church or ministry does not have a logical beginning and ending the way a school year does or normal nine-to-five job. There are events going on almost every morning or evening. The top guy is often expected to be

Figure 3.2. Workaholism is a broken ladder

there. The normal work week is to have Saturday and Sunday off. Not for a person in ministry. Saturday he's preparing for Sunday. So he ends up working seven days a week. If a pastor tried to block out, say, Mondays and Tuesdays as his weekend, people wouldn't get it."[2]

There are many ways a person can try and heal the brokenness underneath. For pastors, workaholism is an approved, affirmed, and encouraged choice.

DOING, NOT BEING

We sometimes refer to intensive counseling, which is doing multiple hours of counseling over a few days or a week, as an emotional crucible. In normal life when we brush up against negative feelings our instinct is to avoid, fix, or medicate, not to dwell on those feelings. In intensive counseling there is the space and the containment to sit for a time with these feelings in order to do some evaluation. What is the fear that I am experiencing really about? What do I usually do with these feelings? What does God have to say to this place inside of me where this is coming from?

In Christian ministry we have the role of bringing the words of life to others. We talk of the soul, the heart, ultimate purpose and meaning. Yet many of us are unaware of what is driving us. We are aware of the good godly motives for our actions, and we are often aware of the sinful motives for our actions, but we often are missing the broken motives for what we do.

Ministry will push all of your personal buttons. The devil will jump on board to make sure you feel every struggle, doubt, and temptation. Many leaders want the silver bullet of ministry performance without realizing the real problems below the surface fueling this desire. The brokenness beneath is what needs to be addressed as well as the root causes of ministry failure. This is what we will look at next.

ALL SHOT UP

Charlie had finally hit a wall after thirty-six years of doing ministry in the fast lane. His body brought the problem to his attention. It was breaking down. For the past eighteen months he had had one medical issue after another. A doctor eventually confronted him and told him he needed to slow down. He tried—he couldn't.

He ended up at Marble Retreat to try and figure out what was driving him. He began to see how it seemed he was trying to work harder than God in his ministry. He stopped at Marble and started thinking about it. He began to plan how his life and ministry would look different.

Fortunately, with eight days of rest and fresh air in the mountains, some TLC, and the first break from ministry in over three decades Charlie was feeling better. Unfortunately, the pain that had been his motivation for change was lessening. By the last day Charlie was chomping at the bit to get back to ministry. He was an addict—a workaholic and he was not quite ready to give it up. "Prop me up beside the pulpit when I die."

REFLECTION QUESTIONS

1. Are you exhausted more often than not?
2. Would the biblical metaphor "spring of living water" accurately describe you?
3. If your body alone was the measurement on how healthily you are doing life and ministry, what is the message it is sending?
4. Have you struggled with equipping yourself as your first go to when facing a challenge?

5. Is it hard for you to rest? To play? To not be constantly writing a sermon in your head or chewing on a ministerial issue?

6. Has discerning between what God asks of you and what you or others place on you become blurry?

PART TWO

PROBLEMS
IN MINISTRY

4

THE FUSE IS LIT

Buck was the senior pastor of a large and growing church. He had been in ministry for twenty years, but he came in for counseling with a question he could not answer. "What is wrong with me?" Buck asked with a hint of desperation and discouragement as he sat down.

"I don't know," I replied. "I think I'll need some more information."

Buck then began analyzing himself, "I am wondering if it is depression, or maybe a midlife crisis, or maybe my testosterone is low. What do you think?" "

"Again, I think I'll need more information," I replied. "How about telling me what's been going on in your life and ministry?"

Buck then began to unpack his last three to four years, which included the following events:

- 💣 an extended church building and fundraising project
- 💣 his sister dying of breast cancer
- 💣 his handpicked associate pastor having an affair with a lead volunteer in the youth ministry

- ◆ a near church split because of fallout from the affair, which included numerous families leaving the church
- ◆ his teenage son taking a walk on the wild side
- ◆ his own diagnosis and treatment for skin cancer

These events fly above and beyond the normal stressors of directing a large church, which include staff and congregation conflicts, hiring and firing, leading the staff team, preaching, funerals, and casting vision.

After Buck finished his list, I asked him if he had taken any breaks during these past three years. The answer was basically no. The "breaks" were usually conferences or adding an extra day on to a weekend when he was traveling to do a funeral in the family. He usually stayed around to help with the after-funeral business that needed to be taken care of.

When counting up the points on a stress list, he was well above the overload zone. His question about "what is wrong with me" is a common one.[1]

What makes ministry so rewarding but so prone to dangers most of us cannot see? We've talked about bullets; we should not forget the explosives that eventually destroy the target—when all the leader wanted was a silver bullet as a trophy for a job well done.

Christian leaders have power and influence, are under stress, and without dealing with their issues, can explode, causing damage to themselves, their families, and their ministries.

Let's go back to the explosives metaphor. Christian leaders are not like dynamite—an explosive that can be volatile and unpredictably will explode when not cared for correctly. They are more like plastic explosives—adaptable, adjustable, moldable, and can be handled roughly without exploding.[2] Until one day when the fuse is lit and the conditions are just right. Or I should say wrong.

With much focus in recent years on moral breakdowns, and mental health issues, one could get the picture of pastors as a fragile bunch, always on the edge. My experience has been quite the opposite—they take a lot of abuse and handle it well for a long time before finally succumbing.

What places pressure on those in the ministry?

DROPPING OUT

In the Christian community the difficulty of the pastoral position and more specifically the reason for the high dropout rate of those in ministry has gotten much attention over the past fifteen years or more. While recent research would suggest the rate of those who leave ministry is not as high as feared, research does confirm that the Christian leader's role is a struggle, and churches in many cases are not doing an adequate job of caring for their leaders.

One research study compared the burnout rate for those in ministry to the burnout rate for those in other emotionally demanding or intense jobs. It found that clergy had moderate rates of burnout. The burnout rate for pastors was relatively lower than for police officers or emergency personnel, similar to the levels of those in the social work or teaching fields, but at higher burnout rates than counselors.[3]

Lifeway Research did a large research project interviewing pastors in the ministry and pastors who left the ministry. Scott McConnell, Lifeway Research vice president, said based on the results, "This is a brutal job." McConnell adds, "The problem isn't that pastors are quitting—the problem is that pastors have a challenging work environment." McConnell estimates a total of 29,000 evangelical pastors have left the pastorate over the past decade, an average of fewer than 250 a month.[4]

While this number is much lower than some of the numbers thrown around for the last decade or two, this shows pastors are stressed and still a good number do leave the ministry affecting them, their family, and the church left behind.

According to Lifeway Research, here are some of the ways pastors experience their role:

- Eighty-four percent say they are on call twenty-four hours a day.

- Eighty percent expect conflict in their church.

- Fifty-four percent find the role of pastor frequently overwhelming.

- Fifty-three percent are often concerned about their family's financial security.

- Forty-eight percent often feel the demands of ministry are more than they can handle.

- Twenty-one percent say their church has unrealistic expectations of them.[5]

Buck represents the typical pastor. He has a lot on his plate, has taken a lot of emotional hits, and is not taking care of himself. Something is going to give. Doctors and authors Joseph Ciarrochi and Robert Wicks write, "What persons in ministry must learn is what therapists have been taught for years, namely, that if balance, distance, a sense of one's own limits, and an appreciation of the absolute need for rest, good food, exercise, and leisure are not present, then burnout is not a potential danger, it is a certainty."[6]

On call twenty-four hours a day and overwhelmed. This is exhausting.

WHO AM I? THE CHALLENGES
OF BEING A PASTOR

I know of four challenges facing the pastor.

Not one of the regulars. Burns, Chapman, and Guthrie, authors of *Resilient Ministry*, capture a huge challenge of the ministry position in their research through The Pastors Summit: "One of the unique aspects of pastoral ministry is how it affects and defines all areas of life. Work, family, and personal responsibilities blur together through the week, so that pastors have difficulty distinguishing when they are on and when they are off duty."[7]

I was at a barbecue for my ice hockey team, and a few of the guys were asking about my job counseling pastors. One of them said, "What is the deal with pastors anyway that they need a place for counseling?" I explained to them how many pastors cannot do what we were doing at that moment—just being one of the guys hanging out, having fun, with no agenda. Sometimes this is the pastor's choice; sometimes it results from people's expectations. Like a flashlight, always being on drains. In whatever way it happens, no one gets to really know the pastor, nor does the pastor have many friendships inside his own church.

All alone. My DMin research found isolation to be the number one contributing factor to struggles in ministry. Burns, Chapman, and Guthrie also found this to be a problem. They have this to say about isolation in ministry and the need for community: "Vulnerability in safe relationships makes learning possible. Therefore, it is not surprising that the isolation and loneliness of ministry often turns hardships into damaging experiences rather than ones of growth. Intimate relationships are necessary for spiritual growth."[8] Hardship plus isolation equals damage.

Can a person fill all these roles at once? Many occupations carry with them the risk of stressing out in a stressful world.

What is unique to those in ministry is the causation of these issues, the context in which these problems occur, and then the context in which the ministry leader is trying to recover. Here are some particulars regarding the context in which many ministry leaders live, especially pastors.

The "glass house" experience, living in a fishbowl. The feeling or reality of being watched. We repeatedly hear stories from Christian leaders of how people in their congregation or ministry make comments about their parenting, the kind of car they own, what they wear, and even their haircut.

Covering our identities. I used to be a hospice chaplain and at the same time I played in a men's hockey league where most of the guys knew of my career. In a playoff game I went into the offensive zone offside and scored a goal. The referee did not see it. Skating past the opponents' bench on the way to my team's bench, an opponent yelled, "The refs didn't see that, but God saw that!" It was a "friendly" reminder that I was seen differently.

Potential loss of who one really is. Can never be "real" with anyone. Being real in this point means being comfortable sharing struggles, pain, sin, or even frustrations with the ministry and those they are ministering to. One challenge in ministry is to know who to share with and who not to, as one dances the tightrope of saying too much. Everyone wants you to be real but being too real can cost you your job.

Personal spiritual poverty. Always pouring into others, not into self. One of the biggest and saddest ironies of being in Christian leadership is how many experience a challenge staying intimate with God. Always studying and reading in preparation to minister to others.

The spiritual battle of being a pastor. Being on the front lines. There is an increased spiritual battle compared with other professions. Satan makes those who take God's word to the nations a direct target. Taking out a shepherd is a strategic move of the enemy to hurt the whole flock.

Cultural pressures and influences such as the breakdown of truth, and secularism. There is a large, underlying cultural shift from historically accepted values and norms to nearly anything is acceptable, from being a production-, work-, and family-oriented culture to being a consumer- and entertainment-driven culture, from a respect of leadership and experts to suspicion of authority and the deification of personal opinion, and changing from a Christian value-based culture to a post-Christian culture.

Omni-competent. The Christian leader and those they lead hope they will be good at everything including preaching, teaching, vision casting, human-resource management, budgeting, recruiting, fundraising, and on and on. A surgeon is expected to be good at surgery. A pastor is expected to be good at everything, probably including surgery if someone in the church needed it.

A conflictual position. For many peacemaking and sometimes people-pleasing pastors the tension in life and ministry leading to an explosion is conflict. Lifeway Research found, "Most expected conflict to arise, and it did—56 percent clashed over changes they proposed, and 54 percent say they experienced a significant personal attack. Yet nearly half (48 percent) say their training did not prepare them to handle the people-side of ministry."[9]

People pleasing and being conflict avoidant go hand in hand. You cannot make people happy with you if you oppose them. And people pleasing is common in pastors. Charles Stone researching its prevalence in ministry found this, "Surprisingly, 79 percent of the leaders in one survey of 1,000 pastors and 91 percent in another survey of over 1,200 pastors admitted to people-pleasing tendencies to some degree in their respective ministries."[10]

On the good side, many pastors are people pleasers because they care about people and those people's desires, opinions, and hearts. On the broken side, many pastors can care too much what people think of them and value too much the approval of others. This working for approval through people pleasing reveals a pastor's own insecurity and how they are bolstering their own ego.

David was a pastor who was trying to stop a church split. He grew up in a home where his father was physically and emotionally abusive to his mother and verbally abusive to him and his brothers and sisters. David had grown considerably in his adulthood in his ability and comfort in dealing with conflict and saw himself as a good team leader with gifts in peacemaking. Yet this church split and particularly the animosity between people on each side was keeping him up at nights. He often felt like he was back in his childhood home and just wanted to leave it forever.

David began to experience real, deep anger at some of the people involved in the conflict yet face to face he stuffed it and acted nice. He used alcohol to cope with the stress and he withdrew from his wife and kids.

Due to the factors that we just looked at, depression can be the resulting experience for many in ministry. In all, 45.5 percent of pastors say that they have experienced depression or burnout to the extent that they needed to take a leave of absence from ministry.[11]

The ministry position is a tough position. Many people underestimate or do not even consider the pressure on a pastor or missionary and on their marriage, if married. The Christian leader is not only dealing with many stressors but can also be the most isolated one in their church or organization. Stress and lack of support can result in an explosion.

pressure + lack of support = explosion

DON'T LEAVE OUT THE PHYSICAL

Newton has a big hand and a big smile. He is the kind of guy most people like immediately. His infectious personality, gifted story-telling talents, and all-around likability have made him one of the most well-known church leaders in the country while leading the largest church in his denomination.

Newton has a problem though. While he is the man with one thousand friends, his family and staff do not particularly like him. To be blunter, they are very exasperated with Newton. The elders were caught off guard when Newton's wife and the executive pastor came to them in desperation saying Newton needed help or there would soon be some serious consequences. Both the wife and the executive pastor were ready to divorce Newton.

The elders were involved because the first challenge was the biggest: Newton does not think he needs help. Both Newton's wife and the executive pastor have tried their best to get his attention, but he is not listening. They needed some leverage and the elders had it—his job.

Newton's wife, Karen, was fed up with his never being home, breaking promises to her and the kids, impulsive spending of money, and his overall irritability. The elders were shocked to hear this as the picture they had was of a loving and devoted husband. When asked, Newton had regularly reassured them everything was good at home. Karen, in protecting her husband, his position, the church, and their marriage, had been quiet.

The staff's frustrations with Newton as communicated by the executive pastor included: Newton's not being available to staff for conversations, Newton's regularly changing the focus or mission of the church just as staff were building momentum on the previous one, and other impulsive decisions which were often contradictory to an expectation he had just laid down. And it wasn't just the staff's feelings about Newton. Newton was very irritable and unhappy with them as well.

As we got to know Newton and got his history it became apparent, at least to us, that he was manifesting many of the symptoms of bipolar disorder. While most Christian denominations affirm the theological truth of the brokenness and imperfection of humanity, some denominations have been slow to accept that physical brokenness or imperfection (body chemistry and brain) can affect one's thoughts and emotions. Often the belief is that one's thoughts and feelings can and should only be addressed and treated in a directly faith-based way, and not in a medical manner. Unfortunately, this has left many Christians and Christian leaders untreated and sometimes even shamed for their lack of faith in dealing with their emotions and imperfect minds.

If a pastor has something like bipolar disorder, this does not mean that they are not called, or not gifted, or not being led by the Spirit. It just means like every person they are bringing their own brokenness into the mix and ideally this brokenness needs to be dealt with directly and effectively with the right intervention.

Newton came for counseling at the imploring of church leadership and his wife. He has a good heart and desires his relationships to be in a good place. For the first few days we got to know Newton he did the usual human maneuver of wanting a way to fix everything without personally changing. When he was ready to get real, he confessed to the daily private battles he fights with his own mind and emotions and the constant regrets he has for things he impulsively says and does. This opened the door to a diagnosis and appropriate effective treatment.

THE THREE BIGGEST ROOT CAUSES FOR THE PROBLEMS IN MINISTRY

I've talked about the challenges to a pastor as compared to the challenges to the business leader. I've talked about the various issues and problems pastors face in the ministry. But in sum, there are three root causes for the problems pastors have in their work and service.

My doctoral research found that the three most common causes of the problems ministry leaders have are *isolation, unrealistic expectations,* and *poor boundaries*. These three "causes" have underlying causes. Why is the pastor living and working in isolation? Who has unrealistic expectations? Others? Why is the pastor giving those expectations influence over him? Why does the pastor have poor boundaries? For the most part, boundaries are wrapped up in yes and no. Does the pastor struggle to say no?

How do you know if you struggle with isolation, unrealistic expectations, and poor boundaries in your life? One word: stress! Constant stress with the accompanying experience of little joy, peace, and confidence in what you are doing. Always in a hurry to get things done.

Isolation is when you are not regularly in the type of community or relationship where you can share your innermost self. Like Elijah, you feel like you are serving God alone.

Unrealistic expectations are expectations that are unattainable. While the conscious motivation may be to aim toward excellence, the end result is often frustration and disappointment or even the shame of not being good enough.

Poor boundaries can be recognized by seeing that others set boundaries for you. Their agenda, desires, or needs dictate what you do and how long you do it. I remember working with a pastor with a very needy person in his church and he reported regularly spending most of his day ministering to this individual. His argument for the lack of a boundary and corresponding frustration and exhaustion was that it was his responsibility to care for his parishioners. My question to him was, "Does spending four hours with this person at a time help more than one hour?" You may have a responsibility to help but you can define it.

Newton struggled in all three of these areas. His bipolar disorder cranked up the struggle. Buck, from the beginning of the chapter, struggled in all these areas as well.

A couple of God-given protections and interventions for pastors' unrelenting pressure are community and boundaries. Many in ministry do not have these. In many situations these aren't available to them.

The pressure grows, the fuse is lit, and the explosion happens.

REFLECTION QUESTIONS

1. Do you have a clear job description? How closely would you say it lines up with how you describe your calling? Your gifting? Your passion?
2. On a weekly basis do you constantly battle what you feel you have to do versus what you want to do or believe are your priorities?
3. Are you constantly frustrated by how much you don't get done?
4. Do you directly experience people's unrealistic expectations? How about your own?

5. Are you regularly satisfied with how a ministry under-
   taking (sermon, program, training, experience) went
   or more regularly dissatisfied?
6. Are you able to set boundaries to get the main things
   done or regularly interrupted and have to take from
   personal and family time to finish up your priorities?

MEGAPASTORS

The Fallout from a Megaton Bomb

M ATTHEW LED ONE of the larger churches in America and was a popular author. He arrived in Marble shortly after detonation and losing his ministry. His marriage was hanging in the balance. He was caught in an extramarital affair. His pressing question to us was the same as everyone in his situation. How did this happen? Why did I do this?

Over the next eight days Matthew unpacked what had happened and how he had gotten to this point, and we began to understand the underlying issues that led to the explosion of his ministry.

Even a pastor caught in Matthew's position goes through the well-known stages of grief—shock/denial, bargaining, anger, depression, and acceptance. Pastors who have just blown up their lives cycle through these, sometimes multiple times, before arriving at a long-term acceptance that it is what it is.

Matthew followed a well-worn trail to moral failure by megapastors. (Typically a church is consider *mega* if there are over two thousand attendees on a given Sunday, and the senior pastor of a megachurch is therefore a *megapastor*.) To oversimplify, here is Matthew's path. Matthew climbed the church's version of the ladder of success. He was intelligent, passionate, a great orator and vision caster. As he climbed, the pressure grew, and while he thought he was handling it well, the constant demand for perfect production was killing his heart and soul. To keep up with the demands he had to be more driven, more than he already naturally was. He stole energy from his hobbies and relationships to put into ministry. He took hours of sleep and sacrificed those on the altar as well.

Because his church was growing, all looked good on the outside and he didn't realize how starving his heart was for something besides ministry work. A young, affirming, empathetic woman on staff began to listen to Matthew. Matthew had the power and freedom to begin breaking all his own boundaries and set up meetings with this young woman. Then he "needed" to have her travel with him. No one asked questions. The slippery slope was set and ended with Matthew hitting the biggest self-destruct button in ministry—the extramarital affair.

Now, megapastors blow up their ministries in other ways than moral failure. Some burn out. Some become toxic. Some "grow" beyond the theology of their denomination and leave seeking greater freedom. Some misuse funds. And there are many megapastors who manage it well and finish strong. Bob Russell is a name that comes to mind of one who did it well. He began pastoring Southeast Christian Church at the age of 22 when it was 120 people and when he retired there were 18,000 attending. What is distinctive about Pastor Russell is not how the church grew under his leadership but how he has avoided scandal and remained humble, as described in his recent book reflecting on his years in ministry and his focus on what he would have done differently.[1]

There are common pitfalls for those in leadership in large ministries that can fuel the bomb and light the fuse. To begin with, a person in leadership has a lot of power and influence. They are typically under immense pressure and through discipline and submission can positively affect many, or their power can get out of control and damage numerous folks.

THE PATH TO DESTRUCTION

When megapastors explode, it does not only impact a small community. Whole blocks are leveled. But why do they explode? Like Matthew thought, *I have arrived, why would I destroy everything I had been working towards?*

One of the reasons pastors of large ministries explode is the pressure to perform constantly. Ironically, performance is often what got pastors to this position in the first place, and now it is threatening to take them out. In the early days, this performance was natural, life-giving, and inspired. As performing becomes more and more expected it can become draining, fear-filled, and rarely enjoyed.

Recent research has found a commonality in personality type among megapastors. The findings from the research indicate a significant relationship between Enneagram Threes (Achievers) and Eights (Challengers) as a common profile of the megachurch pastor (in 79 percent of the cases).[2] It makes sense that these personality types are drawn to and successful in this challenging role. What does it mean for the risk of blowing up? If one's personal brokenness reinforces one's natural gifting and proclivity, then one can be at high risk. Our brokenness, if deep enough, does not add dysfunction to our natural gifting—it multiplies it. Here's the equation:

natural giftedness × personal brokenness = at-risk pastor

If you are a driven, goal-oriented person and you carry with you some form of deep shame or insecurity, then you switch from "desiring" to be successful to "having" to be successful. And when you have to be successful it becomes first in your life. The God-given temperament of achiever goes from being in submission to God and modesty to being in submission to the dysfunction.

This obsession with success can blind a leader to other pertinent information about how their life is going. The leadership of a ministry asked us to do a health assessment of their staff, meaning how they were doing interpersonally because this ministry had a pattern of staff leaving or falling morally. We began by interviewing senior staff. Overall their message was "Everything is going great. We are hitting on all cylinders. We feel good about life and ministry."

We asked to interview their spouses. Overall their feedback was "Our marriages and lives are falling apart. My spouse is rarely home. I am beginning to hate that he/she works for this place because of what it is costing us. We are both exhausted." Christian leaders need to know how they are really doing in their personal lives.

When one makes the "big time" there is not just the pressure to perform, but to do it excellently. The pressure to hit every sermon, every interview, every book, every next vision out of the park every time. When thousands gather to hear the great preaching of so-and-so, then it had better be good. When a megapastor is paid thousands of dollars to speak at a conference, he had better wow.

With the pressure to perform and to be exceptional, the danger of seeking success at all costs can creep in. Pastors can start breaking all kinds of boundaries. They start to believe that they need to figure out ways to squeeze more and more out of themselves. I have worked with pastors where caffeine was not enough anymore so they were juicing themselves up on Adderall in order to run on less sleep. Just so they could be "energetic."

Pastors begin breaking all their own rules of biblical interpretation so they can get a message they think sounds exciting and new. Pastors plagiarize when their own stuff isn't hitting the mark or their creativity has dried up. Pastors terrorize staff to make every service an exceptional one—new stage, more effects, more passionate worship, whatever. The motivation has gone from glorifying God and teaching his Word to blowing people's socks off.

And eventually outright sin can become justified. Regularly when megapastors are caught in sin and are in the shock/denial or bargaining stage they have a lot of justifications for why they needed what they needed. They can be so self-deluded at this point that they convince themselves that the sin was needed to do God's work and since God is blessing their work that is proof it is okay. The lie goes like this: I need (alcohol, pornography, illicit relationship, drug, anger, not prioritizing marriage and family) so that I can do what I need to do as pastor of this church, and that's the most important thing in all of our lives.

When "success at all costs" comes in, then there is no room to be like Jesus. The fruit of the Spirit is not helpful when you must get things done. Pastors who beautifully preach on love, grace, patience, and kindness have little room for them in their own lives. More troubling than the scant evidence of these Christlike attributes is the lack of desire to grow in these character traits. What helps is assertiveness, decisiveness, and action.

And they can begin to believe their own hype. Success is dangerous for a human. We are so prone to pride that when everyone is telling us how great we are, we are likely to believe it.

Megapastors have to stand on diligent guard against pride. Yet, many of them don't fight against it and actually desire the adulation and constant affirmation. They can begin to believe that they are special. Megapastors need to be confident, but this confidence easily crosses into arrogance which opens them up to taking on too much, justifying self-centered behavior, or not respecting God's or other people's authority.

THE ENABLERS

To make matters worse, the church buys in to how great the megapastor is. I am not surprised by the sin of megapastors. They are human and susceptible, which reminds me of a sign I saw on a restaurant wall about preachers: "Preacher's downfall is the 3 g's—the glory, the gold, and the girls." I am sometimes surprised by the extent that those around them do not see and believe the signs that something isn't right and then the lengths they will go to protect them. "All truth passes through three stages. First, it is ridiculed. Second, it is violently opposed. Third, it is accepted as being self-evident."[3] In the case of megapastors who are heading to destruction, often first their acting out is denied or overlooked. Then when someone raises the warning flag the concerns are ridiculed, and then opposed, and finally, if true, it is accepted as being self-evident.

HOW IT PLAYS OUT

All of the above lead to a couple of major problems and put the megapastor at risk for blowing up their lives and ministries. First is the continued erosion of boundaries. Boundaries around self, marriage and family, rest, and their own relationship with God. They don't care for themselves, at least not in a healthy, God-honoring way. Also, their boundaries with temptation can begin to erode whether it's money, alcohol, or the opposite sex. The leader of a huge ministry often exists in a context with no accountability, little oversight, and a whole lot of trust.

And then the temptations are just too hot to handle. The megapastor can easily become emotionally, spiritually, and relationally depleted. He is in pain, he is under pressure to perform, and he has his own personal "fix" to handle all of this. "Then, after desire has conceived, it gives birth to sin; and sin, when it is full-grown, gives birth to death" (James 1:15).

This book has talked of all the challenges and potential pitfalls of ministry. For megapastors these are the same issues, but they are on steroids.

There are many leaders of expansive ministries who fight hard against the dangers of pride, the freedom of no accountability, and the temptations at hand. They battle to remember whose ministry it really is and seriously pursue after Christlikeness. Accountability, protection of the pastor's time and energy through specifying their call and responsibilities, and sabbaticals are a few interventions that help megapastors stay healthy.

And while this keeps them out of some of the pitfalls just mentioned, they are still at risk of failing via burnout. Often the risk comes through their gift of being visionaries. They see what is possible. They cast big dreams. This is largely what helped them launch, grow, or succeed in the opportunity they had. The downside is that they can believe the success of this venture is on their backs and they need to make sure it works.

BACK TO THE HEART OF MINISTRY

Taking some time to reflect, Matthew now saw how he had gotten off track. He fondly recalled his first ministry where it was just Jesus and him sharing the good news and loving on people. He didn't realize how empty, lonely, and driven by the crowd he had become.

He grieved that he had wandered so far from Christ. He grieved how much "serving God" had become about a show and keeping a big company going. He missed the little things, the slower pace, the time to sit with Christ and others.

Matthew saw where he repeatedly rationalized his own weariness by what he was doing for the kingdom and that his now shallow fulfillment had become the attention and applause. He recognized how dangerous "success" had been for his own heart and soul and how he fell hook, line, and sinker for the devil's temptations.

Matthew was now humbled, no longer the man with all the answers. He had been missing the biggest answer himself for some time now—his love for Christ and Christ's love for him. He was now ready to do what Christ asked of him, and it wasn't succeeding in people's eyes. First, was repairing his marriage. This took confession, repentance, humility, and sacrifice. It took putting his relationship with his wife over getting something done.

Also, Matthew began spending a lot of time talking with God and listening. He slowed his pace. He was no longer on the treadmill of performance. He began to see and hear Christ's intimate presence with him again. Matthew stopped caring about nickels and noses and cared about his first love.

Due to his affair Matthew had to leave his church. He even left his denomination. He found a job serving at an inner-city mission that didn't care he had committed a sin in his past. He was unseen and unknown, which was a spiritual discipline as he was used to thousands of "likes" and followers. While this was hard for him in some ways, in others he was more at peace than he had been in a long time. He was walking with Christ and others in an intimate way. Matthew could see Christ in all that he was doing. He knew it wasn't about himself anymore, and he was relieved.

AVOIDING THE MEGATRAP

I feel for those who have hit "success" in the ministry. The pressure is immense, the responsibilities and opportunities are endless, and the expectations are through the roof. In success, we hear everything we want to hear about ourselves—we are important, we are adequate, we are loved and respected, we have power, and we make a difference.

But in success is the danger that we forget who truly makes all of us adequate, important, loved, and effective—Christ. It is only through Christ that we make any kind of real and lasting change and only if we do it in His way.

THE FRUIT OF THE SPIRIT

When we are in Christ, we have his Spirit dwelling within us. What does that look like? Love, joy, peace, patience, kindness, gentleness, faithfulness, gentleness, and self-control, we are told in Galatians 5:22-23. One way to ensure that you are not falling into the megatrap is asking yourself the question: Am I practicing and growing in the fruit of the Spirit? Does our ministry encourage growth in these Christlike attributes or are we about perfection and performance?

INTIMACY WITH CHRIST

The danger of a large ministry is to let ministry dictate how and what we do, not how we walk with Christ. If we find ourselves justifying our lack of prayer time, lack of time and effort toward wife and family, and lack of time in our own personal worship then we are getting the cart before the horse.

Look at your life, and ask if your relationship with Christ comes first, ahead of serving him. Do I go to Christ first for major decisions, or are they ruled by the leadership strategy of the day? Do I sense immense pressure to keep the ministry going, or do I know with great security that in Christ all things work and hold together? Do people leave the church, sermon, worship time, or other form of ministry I lead saying how great I am or how great Christ is?

SET BOUNDARIES AND KEEP THEM

Usually by the time I see megapastors, their lives have exploded and they are ready to be honest, very honest. At times I am dumbfounded by the indiscretions they have been getting away with on the path to destruction, seemingly hoping they would get caught. Financial issues, relational issues, and ministry control issues are areas where they often act out. They report how they blew through boundaries, breaking their own values along the way.

All pastors, but especially those in large ministries, need to set clear boundaries, and there needs to be oversight and accountability. When a megapastor's fame has gone to their own head they will push for more power, more exceptions, more whatever, and there needs to be someone who says, "No!" before the explosion and termination.

HEART CHECKUPS

One of the big lies that fuel the downward spiral of the large ministry leader is the belief that we are okay. This lie is fueled by the evidence of the ministry growing and by other people's affirmations. But in the end, this is like a thirsty man in the desert being satisfied by a mirage.

Taking account of how one is really doing personally—heart, soul, and in close relationships is important. It is critical to have a clear diagnosis of one's own state to move forward with the appropriate intervention.

An accurate diagnosis of one's spiritual and emotional condition can occur in many ways. A counselor, an assessment, an open discussion with spouse and children are all ways to get a picture of how one is doing. Another way is respecting your time off. Your daily, weekly, monthly, yearly, and sabbatical time off needs to be kept.

The commandment most of us break without batting an eye is "Keep the Sabbath." Taking our time off reveals so much about how we are doing. It can give us opportunity to rest and reflect. Whether we allow ourselves to take a break tells us a lot about whether we are trusting God or taking the ministry on our own backs. During time off we can invest in relationships and our own hearts.

WORLD CHANGERS

We have had the privilege of working with many very gifted ministry leaders. Their vision and insight and boldness have been used by God to push the kingdom forward in places where it needed to go. They are inspiring people to be around, and you can see how God clearly blessed them in their personal strengths as well as opportunities.

But it is heartbreaking to sit with them as they anguish over how they just blew up everything they believed they were about: advancing the kingdom and glorifying God.

Megapastors, you have a lot of power and influence. When talents and opportunity are submitted to Christ it is beautiful and wonderful what he can do through you. If that power and influence is largely controlled by your brokenness and with a little help from the evil one—watch out. There is a mess coming.

SPARED AND SERVING

Pastor Lionel had a close call. He was a few years in to pastoring a large church. It had been going well and he was feeling good, maybe too good. He and others noticed he was getting a little too loose with his boundaries in many areas. He was saying edgier things from the pulpit, he was justifying bigger church and personal expenditures, and he was becoming pushier with staff and elders. A longtime friend and pastor of another large church first called him on it. That was enough for Lionel to know it was becoming an issue. He did not want to be another pastor who crashes.

Lionel came to Marble and he quickly realized he had a case of a runaway ego. His success was going to his head and he could speak of all the building rationalizations that were going on in his head to justify his behavior. When he said them out loud, it was convicting him that his heart was heading in the wrong direction.

Lionel made some changes in his life and ministry including incorporating a regular spiritual retreat into his schedule to stay grounded in who he was really serving and why he did what he did. He also set up more accountability around himself for his attitude and actions. Lionel has gone on to continue in his ministry and is doing well.

REFLECTION QUESTIONS

1. Have the size and success of your ministry overtaken the heart of doing ministry?
2. Do you feel the pressure and expectations are constant, unrelenting, and unreasonable?

3. Does your current way of doing ministry still allow you to deeply connect with God and people?
4. Are you justifying some boundary breaking or unhealthy habits in the name of getting the job done?
5. Do you long for a return to simpler and "easier" times?
6. Is your current pace sustainable?
7. Is there room for play and rest in your life? Are you okay with "wasting" time?

6

THE ISSUES
BENEATH THE ISSUES

C HRISTIAN LEADERS OFTEN DO NOT DEAL with the issues beneath their issues, yet they have access to the truth and grace needed to do so. Dealing with these issues would save them from blowing up their lives and ministries.

Pastor Cliff calls our office at Marble and I take the call. He is inquiring about coming to an eight-day intensive, and I ask him what he is coming to work on. He proceeds to tell me he's coming for burnout. He is the senior pastor of a large and growing church, has a young family, and some strenuous marital issues. These are all contributing toward his burnout, he says.

On one hand, Cliff is correct. On the other hand, there is more to the story. He is correct that all the stressors he listed are stressors and can contribute to burnout. The point he is missing is how his own brokenness plays into how he handles these stressors. All the stressors he mentioned are normal—being a pastor of a church is stressful, so is a young, growing family, and all marriages have their challenges. Many do not burn out from these external pressures.

At the beginning of his time at Marble Retreat, Pastor Cliff began to see how his perfectionism played into how he dealt with the normal stress of ministry and family. This placed a lot of extra and unnecessary pressure on him and on everyone around him. "Aha," he said. "We have found the problem. I just need to stop being a perfectionist—I can do that perfectly."

Yet, this was still just a symptom. What was driving his perfectionism? Where did this come from and how did it become his real religion?

Through questions, wrestling, prayer, and reflection he began to piece together how several experiences and dynamics in his life came about to create this way of handling life's challenges. These included factors such as being the oldest child of five, his parents' divorce when he was ten, and the subsequent experience of being raised by a single mom and having a perceived responsibility for the family. He also was placed in leadership positions in the church at a young age, had a few powerful shame-filled experiences of failure, and received a ton of attaboys for successful behavior.

Now, he thought we had gotten to the root of the problem. But had we? We had gotten to some causes, which are helpful to understand and to know where to heal if healing is needed and where to forgive if forgiveness is needed, but these are mostly signs pointing to the core of the struggle. The core of the struggle for Cliff has to do with his identity and a core fear. Wrapped together, these are a fear of being inadequate and failing. Perfectionism appears to be the perfect antidote.

Here is a way to picture what is going on in Cliff. On the surface are his presenting problems, which are the stressors of church, family, and marriage and the corresponding experiences of exhaustion, frustration, and burnout. The next layer down is his driving motivation, which in Cliff's case is largely perfectionism.

Then are the underlying causes for his perfectionism which include family of origin experiences and shame and reward reinforcement. And finally, at the foundation are his root identity issues and corresponding core fears.

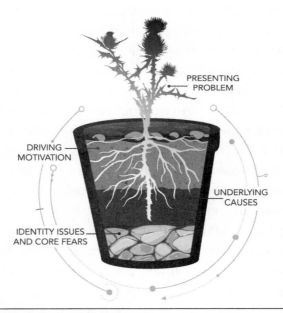

Figure 6.1. Issues beneath the issues

As a counselor, I desire people to be well. As a Christian counselor, I believe God desires people to be well and provides a way for them to be well. In counseling school, I was taught that the issues are never just the issues. Don't just treat the symptoms, treat the cause. Scripture is clear: God is going for dramatic life change in his followers, a change of heart. Jesus talks of this in passages like Matthew 15:18 and Luke 6:45. When God changes your heart, he changes how you see him, yourself, and others. In other words, he changes your identity and takes away fears related to how you once experienced yourself and others.

Christian leaders are people and are just as susceptible as anyone to letting what has happened to them in life, what seems to work, what feels good, to define them. And there are many dynamics within the church and especially within leadership in the church that reinforce not looking deeper at one's own brokenness.

On one level, fear-driven perfectionism was working "perfectly" for Cliff. It was a major player in many of the ways he does ministry, and he was receiving a lot of accolades for how he does ministry.

At a fundamental level, Cliff must wrestle with the question of whether he will let fear-driven perfectionism define how he does life including ministry and relationships or whether he will let God define it. Cliff must answer Jesus' question, "Do you want to be well?" In his case and many others, being well means giving up how he has learned to handle life and succeed. In many ways, perfectionism has become his greatest strength, yet it is soul poison.

Giving it up is difficult. Scary. Humbling. To give up how you do life, your sacred cows of perfectionism and control for vulnerability, dependence on God, and lack of control, is too much for many. They either go back to how they were doing it and throw in a small behavior change—preach forty-five Sundays a year instead of fifty or take an extra day off—or better yet, they find a way to theologically justify the way they are doing it and others who will cheer them on. You can see this in mass at many pastor's conferences. The underlying message of many of the "how-to" workshops, talks, and books is that you can control and succeed in ministry.

Yet, God wants deeper healing for his servants, and he offers it.

The issues beneath the issues are issues of identity—adequacy, acceptance, value and the corresponding fear or shame when our identity is broken. The fear of rejection, the fear of failure, the fear of not being loved, the fear of insecurity. And, of course, the answer for all of these is the cross, the gospel. Christ healed and heals our sin, fear, and shame.

The irony is Christian leaders have the answers to not blowing up their lives and ministry but often are not fully availing themselves to what they are offering to others.

How come pastors do not often deal with the "issues beneath the issues"? They do not because they are pastors and because they are people. Pastors do not deal with the real issues because they are pastors, and pastors do not deal with the real issues because they are people.

BECAUSE THEY ARE PASTORS

If they have an issue, who does the pastor go to for help?

People go to the pastor for that. He has the answers and the faith to deal with life's issues. But if you really want to get to your own issues, you—and the pastor—need someone to walk with you, to ask questions, to encourage, to mirror, to show blind spots, to grieve with, to hold you accountable. The pastor rarely has this person in their lives. When my wife and I had a private counseling practice for eight years north of Denver, many of our clients were pastors. Sometimes I couldn't help but feel some sadness for them. Why? Often a good friend could have played the role I was playing in their life as a therapist. So, here they were in my office—hiring a friend.

And how can a pastor work out their underlying issues, even if they are aware of them? To work on your issues typically means you've got to do things in public others might not like—like going to a therapist. Many pastors feel the danger in publicly working on their own brokenness, weakness, or sin. They know some people may not handle this well, and it could cost the pastor respect or their job. And on the flip side, doing life the way they have been doing it—bulletproof with all the answers—is one of the reasons people like them and pastors often like this about themselves as well.

There are more pastors and churches being open about struggles including mental health issues and the need to get help. You now hear of pastors confessing their struggle with depression and anxiety and sharing that they see a counselor and encourage others to do so if needed. An increased openness and acceptance are needed across the board in churches so more people, including the leaders are safe sharing their hurts and needs. One change I've seen help churches make a shift in the right direction is the addition of a step or support ministry with messages from the pulpit regarding brokenness and the need for healing community.

Another thing that prevents pastors from working on themselves is that it usually takes an investment of time and money, thus they hesitate. They are too busy. This seems selfish. There are so many other ways time and money could be used. Struggling to set boundaries on what other people are asking them to do, they have no time or energy to invest.

I see pastors practicing insanity—wanting something to change in their lives without changing anything. A pastor will come who is experiencing significant burnout and is desperate to get out of the exhaustion, the numbness, the irritability, and whatever else they are experiencing. Yet, when the obvious changes that need to be made are presented, the response is, "I can't do that because . . ." The pastor has bought into a way of doing life and ministry that they are fearful to mess with.

We sometimes joke, rather darkly, that we like working with pastors after they have had a heart attack. Because when suggestions are made for a healthier life their response is, "Yeah, I can do that. I need to do that." But often the forces driving the way the pastor is doing ministry and life right now are so powerful they don't see a way to live life differently or are fearful of what living differently would mean. Sometimes, I feed back to the pastor what I am hearing them say:

"What you are telling me is that you are very burned out from helping people and ministering to others, you want the symptoms of burnout to be gone and for vitality to return, but you don't want to make any changes. Is that correct?"

If they are honest, they will say, "Is that possible? Can you do that?"

Sometimes it is those around the pastor who want them to practice insanity, keep doing the same thing but hoping for a different result. I have had more than one conversation with an elder, mission's director, or bishop, who calls to refer the pastor or missionary to us and in doing so says, "We (the church, mission, denomination) want to send our pastor/missionary to you but we want some kind of reassurance that if we make this investment in them that they will be able to perform better."

"What are you sending them to work on?" I ask.

"Burnout," they reply.

"So, what you are saying is that your pastor is burned out from how they are working, and your hope is that they will return and be able to do more than what they have been doing?"

"Yes."

"Well, I don't suggest counseling, you might try getting your pastor amphetamines instead." (I do not really say that last line but sometimes want to.)

To be fair, many of those in supervisory care for pastors do want them to be well, healthy, and learn better ways to live and work. But there are still a lot of folks in these positions over pastors who think *more is better.*

BECAUSE THEY ARE PEOPLE

"We only change when the pain of staying the same is greater than the pain of changing." There's a lot of truth in that statement. I've been a counselor for over twenty-five years. I'm supposed to help people change instead of staying the same, but the pain is often not enough for change. It does motivate people to want the pain to stop, but not necessarily to change, or at least not change what needs to be changed.

A worship leader came to Marble Retreat and the main reason she came was conflict with other staff. Kamara was "encouraged" to come and knew her job was at stake. It quickly became obvious by her interaction with our staff and other clients she had a level of oppositional defiance. Digging into her past it was easy to see why: an abusive childhood especially at the hands of an over-authoritarian father. She was experiencing pain from the conflicts at church she was involved in and was even more motivated by the fear of losing her ministry, which she dearly loved. Yet, she desired to focus either on the issues of the other people in the conflict or a simple solution, like a tool, to make the problems go away. What she really needed was deep healing from her trauma and an understanding of why she reacts the way she does and a taking of full responsibility for her own reactions. Yet, this is not the path she wanted to take. Why?

BECAUSE IT IS PAINFUL

Profound hurt and wounds drive many of the deeply ingrained patterns of how we act and react. To heal our battered souls and not just get a Band-Aid, we must dive headlong into the pain. A pastor haunted by powerful shame came to see us. He knew the shame came from a lot of sexual brokenness in his youth, and for healing he had to revisit the exact memories he wanted to avoid and bury. It was gut wrenching for him to return to those memories, wounds, and sins. He faced his fears, shame, and personal darkness. He did it with others, not alone. Others "held" and comforted him when he returned to those cursed places. He exposed his personal "demons" to the light of truth and grace, instead of revisiting them with his own shame-filled lies. He allowed Christ instead of the evil one to speak truth. As he said, "I finally experienced Christ as healer." But it is so tempting to not go there. It hurts.

BECAUSE IT IS SHAMEFUL

We can feel emotional pain when reliving past hurtful experiences and we can experience shame when recalling those events that makes us feel *dirty*, *used*, and *less than* in some way. As humans we can experience healthy shame when we admit that we are not perfect, that we are broken, that we are powerless, and even that we are sinful. David knew that he had committed adultery with Bathsheba. He knew he murdered Uriah. Why didn't he face it, and why did he need Nathan to confront him on it? Because David did not want to face who he really was. Even healthy, truthful shame is painful.

With healthy shame we still have a foundation on which to stand—we who are made in the image of God, we who are children of God. David could hear Nathan because his sin did not define who he was. Healthy shame is the realization that we are not perfect, that we are broken, that we fail, and that we sin. Yet it does not take away who God designed us to be. Healthy shame is energizing, convicting, and helping us to want to be more like Christ.

Toxic shame is soul venom threatening even the foundation of who God says we are. When we commit evil or evil happens to us, it is shameful. Then we can believe that even God does not

see us as lovable and acceptable. And we struggle to see ourselves in any other way than how Satan has painted us with sin.
Toxic shame is energy draining. We don't believe we can ever
change, that we can ever be good enough. It causes us to want to
withdraw from God and others and hide.

BECAUSE IT IS CONFUSING

In our minds there does not seem to be a direct correlation between our own deep issues and our current struggle. Kamara, the
worship leader who came for conflictual relationships, could not
see how her abusive dad had anything to do with her negative
responses to staff at the church. Plus, she had the oft-used rea-
soning, "I have forgiven my dad." We are confused because we
are not connecting the dots between the abuse we experienced
and the triggers today. And, unfortunately at times, the church
and Christians have peddled an oversimplified path of healing.

A common avoidance we Christians use is thinking because I
have forgiven him "for what he did to me" it is now having no
effect on my life. This is just not the case. Forgiveness is a step in
healing but in many ways it's separate from working through the
life-altering ramifications the transgression had on you. To oversimplify, if someone hits you with their car and breaks your leg it
is important for you to forgive them, but you still have to deal
with your broken leg. Kamara was broken in ways emotionally
and relationally, and only forgiving her dad would not heal that.

If the wound was traumatic there are many possible ramifications. Often something is traumatic if it was out of your control
(you were powerless), or it caught you off guard (blindsided), or it
was violent or ugly. Some of the lasting psychological effects of
trauma are anxiety, depression, irrational fears, and compulsions.
Emotional symptoms can be numbness, anger, or irritability. And

one can continue to be triggered by stressful or somewhat similar experiences. This triggering not only can cause an overreaction to the current situation but it also continues to keep one physiologically in a heightened state. This can lead to increased blood pressure, adrenal issues, autoimmune problems, and gastrointestinal complications.

BECAUSE IT IS HARD WORK

We all want surgery to be fast, effective, and painless, whether that is surgery of the body or surgery of the heart and soul. We wish there were, but there isn't a magic wand to wave that would take us right to healing. No pill. No bolt of lightning from God. Yet Scripture often shows deep healing (other than physical healing) being a process. Saul did not become Paul overnight and with a flash of light. David shows us in the Psalms the process of working through your struggles and doubts. It is not that people are against hard work, especially most of the Christian leaders I work with; it is just this is not the area they want to focus their hard work on, and they really need to dig in on this aspect of their lives. Many do not see how doing hard heart work helps them be better pastors.

BECAUSE IT DOES NOT LINE UP WITH OUR AGENDA

Many of us, including pastors, do not want to be well. We like our sickness. At least, being well is not high on our priority list. We want to be liked, we want to be successful, we want to be secure, we want to have fun, but we don't necessarily want to be well. And often these other priorities work in exact opposition to being well.

Cliff decided to jump in the deep end. He saw he had deep insecurities and shame about being inadequate, and his fear-driven perfectionism was the antidote he had found. He admitted he was scared. Scared to give up this way of doing life. Who would he be? Would he be good at ministry? Would people reject him? Yet he was tired of living the way he was living, and he knew he was hurting himself and others and not doing it the Jesus way.

Admitting his fear was a huge step. The fear he had in giving up his perfectionism was the biggest and final block to getting well. It was this fear that kicked in every time and told him he needed to perform the same old way, pull out the perfectionism and do what everyone expected, including himself.

We asked Cliff what was the main fear that erupted in him when considering killing his perfectionism. He said, "That I wouldn't be good at anything anymore."

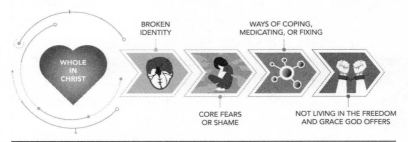

Figure 6.2. Living in wholeness or brokenness

For Cliff, his broken identity or "I am not adequate" belief was the core fear of failure and shame in imperfection. He coped through perfectionism and performance, which led to exhaustion, a ton of pressure on himself and others around him, little to no grace, and a desire to medicate the pressure he constantly experienced. On the outside Cliff was the picture of pastoral success; on the inside he was quickly deteriorating.

Shame, a lie we believe about our worth or identity, feeds our coping strategies, and our coping strategies create problems that negatively affect us and we end up medicating or focusing on these surface level issues. The sum total leads us to not living in freedom.

REFLECTION QUESTIONS

1. What are the surface level symptoms you are wanting to be gone? Exhaustion? Irritability? Guilt? Stress? Fear?
2. What ways of doing life/ministry contribute to your surface experience?
3. Pick a problem in your life in which you play a role and use the five whys technique. For further information on five whys, visit https://en.wikipedia.org/wiki/Five_whys.
4. Is there a prevalent fear or shame-based message that you find yourself regularly thinking? I am going to fail, I am going to be rejected, people don't like me, people don't respect me? Do you know the history to this message? Where did it start?
5. Are there family of origin wounds that contribute to your struggles in ministry?
6. Do you experience freedom and acceptance to be yourself, or do you feel you regularly must act or feel differently for your role or to please others?

7

THE BULLETPROOF VEST

Protection from the Silver Bullet

F RASER COLLAPSED ON HIS WAY to the podium to preach one Sunday. It wasn't a heart attack. It was a panic attack. Up until a few weeks before this he would have dismissed the reality of panic attacks. While he was gracious on the outside in his response to people with anxiety, on the inside he really believed it was weakness.

Fraser was driven. Very driven. He came by it naturally. His father was an acclaimed surgeon and head of a medical school. All of his siblings were doctors or professional athletes. His sister won silver in the Olympics. The family ethic was excelling.

Fraser chose the road less traveled. He was not drawn to the worldly achievements his siblings were. He was looking for something different, something that was meaningful to him. He was always interested in the spiritual side of life, which led him to giving Bible college a try.

Before he left for school, his disappointed father sat him down to give him a lecture on how he was throwing away his future. He heard how Bible college would never prepare him for a decent career, how most young people would love the opportunities he has, and how he could get into any university he desired. Yada, yada, yada. Mercifully his mother interrupted this one-way conversation to tell them dinner was ready.

Fraser found he loved Bible college. He loved the study of Scripture. He loved church history. He loved the art of preaching. He loved engaging with other students who thought, talked, and lived their faith. He loved being involved in something deep and meaningful.

While Fraser chose the road less traveled, he was still driving the family car. Fraser, like his dad and siblings, couldn't just ease his way through college. He took extra classes. He was involved in several ministries. And as soon as he could, he began preaching in local churches on the weekend. He was well liked and well respected and seen as an up-and-coming star. He was the number one draft choice coming out of Bible college.

After an internship Fraser was approached by a couple of elders from a large church whose senior pastor had just left because of moral failure. They wondered if he was interested in the senior pastor position. They explained this was an elder-run church, that they would do the heavy lifting in areas of finances, staffing, and congregational conflict. They promised Fraser that he could focus on preaching, teaching, and writing—his sweet spots and a dream position.

Fraser, not fearing a challenge, took the position even though he was young and inexperienced. He could easily spiritualize that "God doesn't call you where he doesn't provide." Fraser was a high school player drafted for the NBA, his gifting masking his immaturity.

As is often the case in these situations, the church was not nearly as healthy as the elders portrayed it to be, and the elders were not nearly as "hands on" as they thought they were. Once Fraser got in, even a rookie could see there were a lot of problems that were being neglected or mishandled. Always wanting to be "the man," he repeatedly asked for the ball, took more and more of the shots, worked harder to cover both ends of the court, and began taking on coaching responsibilities (leading the elders).

Church, like basketball, is a team sport. While Fraser, like LeBron James of the NBA, can play all positions, he was trying to play all positions at the same time and still come out with the win. His days were getting longer, and his nights were getting shorter. But being young, Fraser was rolling along with this high-pressure life.

Behind every "problem" in a church is someone who cares about that issue. Experienced pastors learn to be patient navigating an issue and making changes when someone in the church feels deeply about the issue, especially if that person has a lot of influence. Even if that issue is the color of the carpet.

A young pastor sometimes only sees the issue and the solution. And while the solution may be correct, a quick and forceful decision to address the matter creates more problems than the problem itself. This is what happened to Fraser on several issues. He boldly made some decisions and messed with some sacred cows at the church. To instigate change and growth he changed Tuesday night Bible study to family night, he hired a decorator to update the sanctuary and in doing so some old donated pictures were removed, and he shot the mother of all sacred cows—the worship style. Now on top of the already stressful situation he was in, there was a growing church split— those who wanted him to stay and those who wanted him to go.

Fraser was in new territory—not being liked and his decisions not being approved of. So add another challenge to his plate—trying to fix the growing dissension between those in the church who saw him as the bright hope for the future and those who saw him as the one gutting everything good from their past. His staff and elders were split as well. His team was fighting in the locker room before they even got on the court.

BURNOUT

Burnout. The result of doing too much for too long. Or doing the wrong things for the wrong reasons. Or living under unrelenting pressure from self and others that steals the joy, peace, and confidence from doing the Lord's work. These are several common paths to burnout, while every Christian leader's journey to burnout is unique.

Comedian and actor Lily Tomlin has a quote that I am fond of using: "The problem with the rat race is that even if you win, you are still a rat." I use this often in our counseling intensives with pastors. I mean no offense by it. Just another way to poignantly and perhaps humorously state that the real question many pastors need to be pursuing is not, How do I excel in ministry? but, Am I pursuing after ministry in the right way at all? Or, Is the goal of improving at ministry actually more about me than what God desires me to do?

Spiritual formation is growing in popularity. More Bible colleges and seminaries are offering courses and majors in this field. As more pastors are being exposed to the disciplines of intimacy with God, they are changing from frenzied, production-oriented ministry lives to slowing down to holy rhythms. There is hope that change is coming.

BULLETPROOF VEST

There are three main interventions to avoid the ministry rat race or to protect yourself from the silver bullet of trying harder: (1) Don't add stuff to your calling, (2) continually keep your relationship with God as a priority, and (3) know your own issues twisting the ministry God called you to and address them.

WHAT HAS GOD CALLED YOU TO?

One of the first pastors I counseled came because of anger issues. The leadership at the church he was serving told him he needed to get help. We quickly got to the core of his anger and it was this: Why did God call me to preaching but not gift me in preaching? He was envious of other preachers who were gifted. He was envious of churches that were growing.

There is a long story to how he came to believe he was called. This pastor was miserable and was placing intense pressure on himself to be Andy Stanley. He was pursuing many avenues to become the megapastor he wasn't, and all this internal angst was leaking out on those around him, especially those he was supposed to be leading, teaching, and encouraging. If a pastor does not have peace with who God has called him to be, how can he lead others to peace?

The topic of "calling" is a complicated one. It varies with denomination, with generation, with personality, with specific church, and with community. There are many good books that wrestle with the topic of calling. But one of the primary causes of burnout is when we place additional burdens on ourselves God has not placed on us. That he has called us to something we just don't believe we can do.

Here are some of things we can add to the call:

- 💣 making ministry about us, putting too much pressure on ourselves

- making ministry our therapy—trying to get unmet emotional and identity needs met through ministry
- adding in our own pet projects
- perfectionism—going beyond excellence to control
- savior complex—I need to rescue and fix others
- avoiding our own personal, familial, and marital brokenness through ministry

There are many benefits to being clear on your calling:

- can make clear and confident decisions regarding different opportunities
- can more easily set limits and boundaries between ministry and personal life
- can become excellent at what you are called to
- can be in your sweet spot more of the time
- can delegate better, which is better for the church, the body

Acts 6 gives us a great example of sticking with your calling and delegating. In Acts 6:1-4, the apostles chose to "give their attention to prayer and the ministry of the word" and turned over caring for the needs of widows to others. Also 1 Corinthians 12 is very helpful in confirming that each person in the kingdom has different kinds of gifts, service, and work. Each person, including the pastor, is a part of the body. First Corinthians 12 reminds us that the pastor does not need to try to be the whole body.

KEEPING YOUR RELATIONSHIP WITH GOD A PRIORITY

Everyone knows this. Everyone preaches this. Everyone believes this. Yet it is a challenge to do it. At least those who are blowing up are not doing it. The main reason? Because ministry gets in the way, ministry becomes a substitute for a close walk with God, ministry becomes rationalized as "this is my way to be close to God," and ministry becomes the most important thing in my life.

It always concerns me when I hear a pastor say, "I feel the closest to God when I preach." On one hand it is good to feel God's closeness and his pleasure when we are serving him. As Eric Liddell said in the movie *Chariots of Fire,* "God made me fast, and when I run, I feel his pleasure."

On the other hand, serving in ministry is a part of our walk with God, but it is not the totality, not even close. I worked with a pastor who was known for his excellent teaching/preaching on sexual issues. The products (book, podcasts, sermons) from his teachings were very successful. As a counselor working with men, I utilized his materials. They were excellent. The only problem— he was having sex with women in his church who were not his wife. This pastor was able to do ministry very well, but his life was far from God.

Herein lies another danger of putting ministry over relationship with God: if ministry is going well (growing, positive feedback, people are being moved emotionally and financially) that must mean God and I are good. Instead of looking at how is my walk with God? Am I being holy as he is holy? Am I loving others? Am I experiencing an Abba and child relationship with God, or is he more like my CEO?

BENEFITS OF KEEPING YOUR RELATIONSHIP WITH GOD FIRST

When we walk close to God, we realize that ministry is not about us, it is about him and we are dispensable. We also focus more on being and not so much on doing. Christian leaders have the tendency to become a frazzled, hurried bunch of folks running on adrenaline and caffeine.

Being in the presence of the Holy One tends to convict us of sin and even convict us when we are tempted to sin. Those who are acting out in ways they shouldn't are typically avoiding personal time with God.

When we spend daily, intimate time with the Father we prayerfully place those people and challenges that weigh on us in his hands. We experience true relief in knowing the Father has heard us and cares.

Perhaps most importantly, when we keep our relationship with God a priority, we remember what it is all about—our first love. We view our ministry as a privilege, rather than a burden.

LIFE STAGE/ PERSONALITY/ THEOLOGICAL INFLUENCES

People go through stages in adulthood that directly influence how we do our career life. In general, we flow from the early stages of building and achieving in our twenties, thirties, and forties into the later stages where we desire to focus more on meaning, depth, and relationship. Or in simpler words we shift more from doing to being. While there may be more emphasis on doing than being earlier, the foundation of our doing should still be out of our being. Christ was in his thirties when he did his public ministry. He was busy but he was always grounded in his relationship with God and was deeply connected to others.

You could get the picture that it is only the type A, driven pastor who burns out. But this is not so. We see all personality types and ministry roles wrestling with burnout. They may have different motivating factors for taking on too much, but they end up in the same place. Overburdened. Exhausted. Depleted. Those that are more pastoral burn out from taking care of others and not themselves. Those that are visionary or teachers burn out from beginning too many projects and programs. Those that are managers burn out from not delegating and getting into too many of the details.

In our counseling we often discuss the distinctiveness of our personalities, whether using the Myers-Briggs, Enneagram, or DISC inventories. While some personality types may be more susceptible to burnout, we have seen all types find their way there. What is most important is for each pastor to discover what is my personal brokenness or motivation that leads me to take on what is not mine to take on.

Another interesting facet in the commonality of burnout among pastors is the effect of theological tradition. Because we serve all Christian denominations, we see folks from strong Calvinist persuasions to strong Arminian beliefs to every shade in between. One could surmise that theological persuasion could be a factor in contributing to or protecting from burnout, but that is not what we have seen. To say it clearly—a person's personal brokenness will influence the broken way they do ministry more than anything else.

If there is not commonality in ministry role, personality, or denomination/theological position in determining risk for burnout, are there other common indicators? Here are a few shared characteristics I see in those who struggle (admittedly this is not based on definitive research but on recalled conversations with hundreds of Christian leaders): sabbaticals not taken or offered, no regular hobby, poor physical health and little activity, full amount of weekly and yearly time off not taken, bulk of responsibilities do not line up with personal gifting or passion, and church and/or staff is conflictual or toxic in some way.

If there is truth in this list, then the inverse would be true as well. Pastors who take sabbaticals, take their time off, work largely in their areas of strength, take care of themselves, have a hobby, and are not stuck in a toxic environment will largely be more protected against burnout.

KNOWING YOUR ISSUES AND DEALING WITH THEM

If it is true that we are both sinner and saint, that we are both royal priesthood and ordinary broken rebels, then it is true that this both/and is present in our ministries. And it is true that ministry and Satan will play on the broken part.

One way to know our issues is to be close to God. His Word, his Spirit, and his holiness can all hold up a makeup mirror and reveal the blemishes. In my life the most regular place my conscience has been moved by the Spirit to reveal sin or needed change is in my quiet time with God. A memory of something I said or did will come to mind with conviction. A Scripture will challenge me. I will catch myself thinking in some ungodly way and be challenged to think of the situation or person biblically.

Another way to know our issues is by being close to others. Having one, two, or more who we really open up to, who really know us, who have the freedom and invitation to tell us like it is, can reveal so much about ourselves.

And we can do our own work. We can take the time and space to do a forensic examination of our hearts and souls. We can ask the questions of why do I do the things I do the way that I do them? What family ways of doing things do I still do? What changes are hard for me to make? We can follow the windows that emotions open to see where they lead. Why do I get angry or frustrated when this happens? Why do I feel depressed or sad on this day? What is the source of this anxiety or fear that I battle? That emotional good feeling that I just had, what caused it? Is that good or bad?

We can take inventories and assessments. We can see a coach or counselor. There are many ways to learn about ourselves and what drives us. Why do we procrastinate? Why do we avoid conflict? What makes our soul sing? The important thing is that we do it and not only spend time on doing, but on learning who we are. Focusing on only doing is like only driving a car and spending no time on maintenance or fixing any inherent flaws or developed problems from driving.

Get help, reach out, read and research about your issues. If you struggle with fear, figure out why. If you have depression, learn about depression and its causes and treatments. If it is pornography, pursue a fix like it is cancer, because it is. Become an expert on your issues.

I have found personality assessments helpful for others and myself in understanding temperament, gifting, and ways of engaging with relationships, conflict, and problems. I have also found other inventories on topics such as burnout, codependency, people pleasing, and others to be insightful. Being in close community with others can be very revealing about who we are. Being in support groups and leading support groups continue to show me how I react to others and what that says about me.

Sometimes the community I engage with are those from the past via their writings. I have gained much in self-knowledge and areas of growth through reading great Christian writers including Thomas á Kempis, Bonhoeffer, Spurgeon, C.S. Lewis, Kierkegaard, George McDonald, and Dallas Willard. Their delving deep into writing on living the Christian life shines light on my heart, soul, and mind. Several books specifically on understanding yourself that are helpful are Viktor Frankl's *Man's Search for Meaning*, Virginia Satir's *Your Many Faces*, and David Benner's *The Gift of Being Yourself: The Sacred Call to Self-Discovery* and *Soulful Spirituality: Becoming Fully Alive and Deeply Human*.

Like many young pastors, I came into ministry ready to prove myself, needing to prove myself. My first full-time professional ministry was as a hospice chaplain. In training they taught me about the "ministry of presence." While I listened, internally I was thinking, "Nope, I am going to have a ministry of action." On a surface level I interpreted this as acts of love for the terminally ill. On a deeper level what I really believed was that I needed to get everyone saved before their death. Much of my motivation was good, and overall most of the people I ministered to would say they experienced being loved and cared for. But my agenda to get them saved produced two main side effects in me. First, it was a lot of pressure! I tried hard to not transfer this pressure on to the person I was meeting with, but I felt it with every visit. What angle do I need to take? What conversation will open their heart? What verse should I read? What prayer should I say?

An interesting corresponding effect was that my approach inhibited my ability to grieve. There were already facets of my background that made grieving a challenge, and I was changing the main component of my relationship with the dying into a performance engagement: Was I doing the right things to help them to accept Christ? And the answer to that question was what influenced me most, not my natural engagement with them.

I was working the angles, I was watching people die and was unable to grieve, and I was being deeply affected by something out of my control—their receiving Christ. It didn't take long for all of this to catch up to me. I can still remember where I was sitting in my car in Peoria, Illinois, twenty-five years ago when I hit the wall. After a particularly difficult death of one of our patients that day, I was in my car sobbing and crying out to God. "I am going to quit! I don't have what it takes to be a chaplain! I can't do this anymore."

In the silence as my pain and desperation hung in the air, I heard God say as clearly as I have ever heard him speak, "You don't have to do it anymore, Mike. I save people. You don't. Get over yourself." (Yeah, I know, "Get over yourself" doesn't sound very godly, but it was exactly what this young, proud chaplain needed to hear.)

I began a journey into what it means to minister to others through Christ and not through my own agenda. I began a journey into how I could fully and freely love others without performance. I began to learn there is a lot of wisdom and a lot to be said for the ministry of presence.

FACING THE DIVIDED SELF

Fraser's ministry drove him relentlessly, and before his collapse he got much applause for it, except from those whose sacred cows he was shooting. Except for his struggle in the area of handling church conflict many would say he was doing it right. He was pursuing every opportunity and in many ways was doing it with excellence. Why did he end up behind the stage in the fetal position?

Fraser was driven by more than his call and his desire to serve God and the church well. In his mind, he had to succeed. Deep down there was a drive and desire to show his family and himself that he had not made a wrong choice and that he could be successful. In a sense he was still trying to make his dad proud, or at least not disappointed.

And though Fraser pursued something different from others in his family, he still went about ministry in the same way they pursued medals and careers. He had to be the best and failure was not an option. To add to the mix, Fraser was a people and relationship person. So when people didn't like him or approve of him, he interpreted this as failure. His reaction to this experience of failure was to work harder. Underneath it really ate at him when some did not like or agree with how he was doing things. Fraser did not deal with the emotional pain of others' disappointment in him. This was his private battle.

There was a growing divide between the person Fraser presented on the outside and what he was feeling on the inside. The greater the divide, the more shame he felt about sharing it with someone. To confess all of his doubts, struggles, hurts, and insecurities felt to him like admitting failure. And admitting failure was like having the house of cards he created of confidence, faith, and being the fix-it guy tumble down.

Fraser did not ask for help. As a self-made man, asking for help meant weakness and that he couldn't do it. So he didn't turn to the elders, he didn't turn to wise folks in the church, he didn't call one of his former professors or fellow Bible college students.

The tipping point was preaching. He was a good preacher and he knew it, so he didn't have insecurities there. But what tormented him was that while he was preaching he was looking at a number of faces of those who disapproved of him. He could see their scowls. He could guess their thoughts. Here he felt more strongly than anywhere this gulf between the external confidence he was portraying and the internal insecurity he was feeling. He desired to experience joy and freedom in preaching, but it was like torment. He desired to freely love those who were disapproving of him, but really he felt anger and hurt. He started to fear having to preach.

He first began to notice the anxiety when he was doing sermon prep. Then as he got closer to preaching. Then as he was walking up to preach. He also noticed that he was exhausted afterwards instead of invigorated like he once was.

STEPS TOWARD HOPE

Fraser arrived at Marble with his tail between his legs. His confidence was shattered. He doubted his call. He wanted to run from ministry since he felt so much shame. He went from rookie of the year to benchwarmer at best. He felt humiliated about his panic attack and having to admit he couldn't do it. Couldn't run the court, be the man, lead the congregation in the way he believed they needed to be led. Wondered if he should just get out.

We followed the rabbit trails into his heart, soul, and mind. What was it that burned him out? What was creating the drivenness? Why couldn't he set limits? When he began to realize he was in over his head, why couldn't he reach out for help? What are his life values/work values? How does he deal with emotional pain? How does he deal with not being able to do it all or have everyone like him? Where did doing ministry like this come from? Himself? Expectations of others? His family of origin?

Fraser began to see that his family had issues with anxiety. While always seeing his family as strong and above emotional weakness because of what they accomplish, he now saw the compulsions, the drivenness, and the control that many in his family displayed. He realized he had been offered a way of doing life he fully embraced as a better way than other people did it, but it was broken.

While here, we saw that Fraser loved God and loved the ministry. One of the healthy, driving forces in his ministry was that he desired to serve God and the kingdom well and was willing to sacrifice. He spoke articulately and often naturally encouraged others in the group with his godly, biblical wisdom.

Those in therapy with him pointed out that while he put himself into an impossible situation, this was also a cause for hope. If he didn't do ministry like he is in overtime in the championship game, then maybe he could love it and be used by God. They affirmed him. They challenged him to give himself the grace he gave others. Fraser began to experience the burden lifting. He began to see himself more clearly. He began to realize that God's expectation of him was very different from his own. He began to have hope that it could be different.

The church didn't want to lose a possible all-star, so they took him back. He told them about his counseling and retreat. He shared what he had learned about himself. There were enough people there who believed in him and liked him to give him another chance.

The first step was a meeting with the elders to explain what things were really like on the inside at the church. The second step was a reclarification of Fraser's roles. The third step was that he and the elders prioritized the hot-button issues in the church and put them in three categories—deal with it now, deal with it later, don't worry about it. (Mrs. Johnson has always complained about the worship being too loud.) With the issues like changes to their programs, an elder or elders were put in charge of dealing with handling the transition and communication so Fraser was not the only target for those frustrated by change.

The fourth step was a care team including an elder, a contemporary congregant, and a retired pastor set up to meet with him weekly to see how he was doing. Was he taking on too much? Was he taking his time off? What did he need to succeed in a healthy way?

I spoke with Fraser about a year later and he was doing great. He was loving ministry. He was excelling as a preacher. He could sleep at night. While he still had to fight the old impulses to take on more, he now knew that he had a choice. He didn't have to take on more—not to please his heavenly Father, not to please his earthly father, not to please himself, and not to race the rats.

Jesus Christ came to set us free. This includes those of us in ministry! Not just free from sin, but free from shame and fear and the need to perform. We are no longer under the law, but under grace! Fraser moved from pressure-filled performance to serving out of confidence and freedom in his call. This allowed him to not take on as much, to be freer about how things turned out, and to enjoy ministry.

God wants you to flourish in ministry. He desires that you shed the burdens you have added to your call and live freely for him and the church. Define your call. Live in your call. Let others pick up responsibilities at the church. And remember: it is God who saves people, not you.

REFLECTION QUESTIONS

1. Can you in a sentence or two define your personal calling in the kingdom?
2. Are you excited about this calling? If not, why not?
3. What have you or others or your position added to your calling? When you add more what is the driving motivation?
4. Do you know your gifting? Personality? In what ministry roles and contexts do you thrive?
5. What would be your dream ministry? What would you be doing?

8

CONFESSION

P ASTOR FERGUSON WAS GOING TO BE a handful. The senior
leader of his board had called us to make the referral. He let
us know Ferguson would be coming to work on the reasons
behind why he had misappropriated funds and had been abusive
to staff through his anger and control. Most importantly, the
senior board member also wanted me to know that Ferguson was
not at all repentant and was blaming others for his mistakes.

When I spoke with Ferguson to do the intake, it was confirmed:
he was a handful. Articulate, assertive, domineering, and working
to be in control of the conversation all the time. Yet he verbally
committed to working on himself; whether he meant it or knew
his position was at stake, I don't know, but I accepted him into
our program.

In therapy he picked up where he left off on the phone call—
trying to desperately stay in control and defend himself from any
culpability regarding the accusations being levied against him.
Phrases like, "Everyone knew exactly what I was doing, I didn't
hide anything." "At the end of the day I am head of this ministry
so I have the right to choose what to do with the money. Do you

realize how much pressure I am under?" "I am the one asking for donations and people give because they believe in what I am doing." "Five thousand people come to that church. If I wasn't there, it would be three hundred." "The church brings in over $10 million a year. I think I am entitled to 10 percent." "I am just a passionate person. No one used to mind my style and now everyone has become all touch-feely suddenly." "If people would do what I ask them to the first time, I would not get upset."

One aspect I do not like about the field of counseling and psychology is the interpreting of everything, including theories on where people choose to sit and what that means. We were three days in and were trying to care for Ferguson. Whenever someone works so hard to protect themselves from any mistakes, sins, or weakness it means there is a very insecure, hurting, fearful person behind the façade. Using empathy, questions, and challenge, we were working on finding a way to the pain under the surface in Ferguson. I had been challenging him in the moments leading up to one of our breaks. When we do group counseling the group members consciously or subconsciously leave the chairs at the head of the room for my wife, Kari, and me.

It communicates in some way that they recognize we are leading this experience. Before break Ferguson was sitting along the side of the room, when we came back from break Ferguson was sitting in "my" chair. While I am not into psychoanalyzing where people sit, the message was clear, Ferguson was taking over the group session.

Group counseling is an interesting beast. It is not always best to immediately intercede when you think it is heading in a dysfunctional direction. Sometimes it is good to let it go for a few minutes and see what happens. I sat in Ferguson's seat and the show began. Ferguson began a diatribe on how the church needs strong leaders, on how pastors are getting soft, on how when you are called and empowered like a prophet you have to step on toes and blow through social conventions. As he got into role his volume went up, his words came out faster, and he was turning red.

I was watching the others in the room. As could be expected they were getting annoyed and frustrated. When I made eye contact with some of them, they were saying with their eyes, "Come on, do something." Another aspect of group counseling is that it is often more powerful for the group members to say something to each other than the professional leaders, so sometimes you wait to see if someone will step up.

What caught me by surprise was that the person showing the most agitation in the room at Ferguson's antics was his wife. She looked like a boiling kettle ready to blow. Inside I was cheering her on, *Come on, say it, say it, say what you want to say*. As if she heard my internal dialogue she yelled, "*Enough!*"

It caught everyone off-guard, including Ferguson, because up to this point she had been very quiet. In the next moments we all witnessed a miracle. A quiet church mouse of a woman became a lion. She grabbed Ferguson by the throat, at least emotionally, and launched into a monologue that would make Meryl Streep proud.

"Ferguson! Stop your talking! I have had enough. Enough! No more! No more lying! No more denying! No more pretending! We both know that you have done things that you shouldn't have. We both know that this money is not yours, or ours. You know that you have a bad temper and you hurt people. You have hurt me! And I am tired of it. I am tired of keeping the lie. I am tired of living in the dark. Ferguson, these people are here to help us, and we need help. Are you going to get honest so they can help us or not?"

Inside, I was thanking God. The intercessor had come in the form of a quiet wife with the roar of a lion. I did feel bad for Ferguson. He looked like a puddle of a man now. He didn't say anything the rest of that day. But the next day he came in and began quietly. His quiet was as powerful as his wife's loudness. First, he apologized to his wife, then he apologized to the rest of the folks in the group, and then he stated, "I am ready to work, I am ready to get help, and I am ready to be honest." He began telling his story—the real story.

In the days that followed Ferguson shared details of his inappropriate actions, more than anyone knew was going on. But he also shared his guilt, his fear, and his shame. And he shared about his childhood and hardships he experienced. Our host couple says that they can tell when our guests are experiencing healing. They say, "Their faces change, they walk lighter, and the light comes back into their eyes." Through confession Ferguson unburdened himself, and he opened himself up to true healing and real help. He was still Ferguson at times and made narcissistic statements, but overall his focus had shifted from self-protection to increasing vulnerability. Through confession he had taken on the demon that had a hold on him, and he was winning the battle.

And he didn't sit in my chair anymore.

CONFESSION IS NOT ONLY FOR THE OFFENDER BUT ALSO FOR THE OFFENDED

Trish had her head down when we walked into the room on the first morning. She stared at the floor for most of the day. She did not laugh at my corny jokes or nod in empathy as others told their stories. But eventually it was her turn to talk and she knew she needed to talk or leave. She probably was wishing she could leave.

She began, not with her story, but with a harsh self-indictment. "I am a terrible person," she said while still not making eye contact. Wanting to understand Trish and how she arrived at that conclusion, we asked her to go on.

Trish decided to jump right in and get the worst over with: "I am the missions pastor and was fired for having sex with the senior pastor." She began to sob, still unwilling to look at the therapists or other group members in the eye.

Slowly over the next few days she began to trust us, she began to believe we were safe people, she began to want to get well. Unfortunately, her story was one we have heard before.

Trish was fresh out of Bible college. A young, passionate, intelligent woman, Trish was hired by a large church to be their missions pastor. She was all in and loved it. She lived at the church, sometimes literally. This constant presence gave opportunity for the senior pastor and Trish to rub shoulders frequently, first metaphorically. Then not.

The senior pastor showed an interest in Trish and her ministry. He was quick with compliments and pledges to support whatever she needed to be successful. She felt supported, cared for, believed in. Yet Trish was naive. She was clueless that the senior pastor had other intentions. Maybe he didn't at first, who knows, but soon he began moving closer to Trish physically.

It began with a grazing of her hand with his, a touch on the shoulder, a hug. At first, she was uncomfortable with this change, but she rationalized it and told herself it was harmless and in her own head. *He is the senior pastor, he is happily married, he is a man of God*, are thoughts she had to maintain her image of him. Then one evening after an embrace, he kissed her. This was enough to blow through her rationales. Trish told him to stop and that this had gone far enough.

Trish's naiveté was about to get blown up. The old saying, "As it always has been, still now is the truth, the sweeter the tongue, the sharper the tooth," was confirmed in the next few minutes. The senior pastor responded to Trish's verbal boundary with threats to fire her and throw her under the bus by telling others that she came on to him, to statements of adoration of how he was in love with her, how beautiful she was, how he loved her and not his wife.

It is hard to put into words the amount of power the senior pastor holds in a situation like this. He is an older man, an authority figure. He is her boss. He is Trish's spiritual authority. He is the one holding the influence and resources for her ministry success. And he has perfected his manipulation. Unfortunately, likely because there have been many before Trish on whom he has honed his skills in getting what he wants.

Trish was confused, scared, and silent. She did not tell anyone. And as could be expected, he pushed the advances, all the way until they were sexually intimate. He continued finding power and control through threats or promises, through compliments or insults.

When a group member asked Trish the glaring question, "Why didn't you tell anyone?" they tapped right into a deep source of her shame. "Why didn't I tell anyone?" She sobbed. "What is wrong with me? Why was I so weak?"

THE PRACTICE OF CONFESSION

We believe in the biblical practice of confession. Most Christians do not practice confession within formal church. It doesn't happen during Sunday morning worship. Even if a church is of the size and inclination to have an open time of sharing prayer concerns, confession almost never happens, unless it is confession of someone else's sin! Most people stick to the safe topics of health and job or concerns for their kids. Most denominations do not have a practice in place to facilitate admission of sin. Those who are not in full-time ministry sometimes practice confession privately with their pastor or sometimes naturally with a friend while hanging out fishing or over a beer.

A congregant can feel unsafe confessing in public. But how much more unsafe it is for the pastor or the pastor's spouse to publicly confess a sin or struggle. The pastor knows his job could be at stake if he opened up about his sin. Once again, there are external and internal pressures for the pastor to stay quiet and isolated and to depend on self to be the confessor and the confessee for themselves.

In the area of sin, being one's own sounding board is especially dangerous. "We are only as sick as our secrets" is a formidable truth. Keeping our struggles to ourselves is like hiring a thief to guard the bank vault. Practicing social distancing with our sinful self may stop the spread but we are still infected. By not confessing, not only does the pastor miss out on an opportunity for an intervention in his struggle, he also misses out on the potentially healing experience of confessing to the body.

Yes, wisdom and discretion must be used by the pastor in choosing the person to whom they confess, but confess they must.

STRUGGLES, DOUBTS, FEARS, AND SHAME

When we speak of confession, we mean confessing sin, but we also mean confessing struggle, doubts, darkness, hurt, fear, and shame. All those things are so often kept inside. Regularly in our counseling intensives a Christian leader begins a point or a story he or she is about to make with these words, "I have never said this to anybody . . ."

It is sad to think that many in ministry do not feel the permission to share their struggles. It is not safe to share their struggles. They carry the weight of hearing the sins and struggles of others yet do not get a chance to unburden themselves. As our culture changes, it is becoming more permissible for younger pastors to share their struggles, but it is often not in a helpful way or in a healing environment.

Scripture is clear about the benefit of confession and the command of confession. But like no longer honoring the Sabbath, many have let it go because confession in church would be like working out at a gym. If we fostered confession in church, we might all have to do some heavy lifting, and it is so much easier to hear about others doing heavy lifting. This is a tragedy as confession done with honesty and vulnerability and received with grace, forgiveness, and understanding is tremendously healing.

Scripture is clear that if we confess we will be forgiven (1 John 1:9). And if we confess and pray for each other we will be healed (James 5:16).

All Christian leaders need to confess for all have sinned and fallen short of the glory of God (Romans 3:23). Confession should be part of the Christian leader's spiritual life just like Bible reading, prayer, or Communion. Many Christian leaders just say "I confess to God" and call it good.

LEARNING TO CONFESS

The first hurdle for the Christian leader is to learn to confess. Many have learned so well to keep their secrets to themselves it is scary just to consider confessing a sin to another.

And confession can be healing—very healing. If we share our sins at all we often come to it in a casual or sometimes hasty manner. Did it, forgiven, move on. Like it is eating kale or having our teeth cleaned. We miss that confession can open us up for a heart transplant, not just a daily aspirin. Confession can be transformative, if it is safe. There is sometimes the need to confess in an unsafe context when our backs are against the wall, but for sharing our sin to be healing, those we share with must handle with care.

And we must be clear about what we are confessing. Not a general statement, like when we make our profession of faith. David wrote, "Then I acknowledged my sin to you and did not cover up my iniquity. I said, 'I will confess my transgressions to the Lord'" (Psalm 32:5). Sounds like David had a running list in his mind of his transgressions.

We must own up our moral failures with a broken and contrite spirit. "My sacrifice, O God, is a broken spirit; a broken and contrite heart you, God, will not despise" (Psalm 51: 17). We read in 2 Corinthians 7:10, "Godly sorrow brings repentance that leads to salvation and leaves no regret, but worldly sorrow brings death."

In addition to being clear on the sin you are owning and sharing, it also heals the effects committing the sin has had on you. The shame, the fear, the questioning of self or God, the regrets, the "how could I's." Self-pity—"I can't believe I did this." Or personal embarrassment—"What are others going to think about me now?" Shameful regret—"I will never be able to forget what I have done." Unbelieving guilt—"I can't forgive myself."

Confession is not math. It is not an experiment with controllable outcomes. It is jumping off a cliff with grace as one glider wing and forgiveness as the other and hoping to fly but expecting to crash into the ground of consequences and guilt. We are promised forgiveness when we confess our sins, and I believe God wants us to fly.

We have seen powerful moments of healing when someone confesses. We were working with a Christian recording artist who had acted out so much sexually you would think he was touring with AC/DC, not The Church Boys (not their real name). After he disclosed some of his sin, I asked him how saying it out loud was affecting him. He responded, "I see now how I have become what I despise. I am one of 'those guys.'" While there was shame in the mix of what he said, more powerfully there was godly sorrow and a penetrating revealing to him of how far he had drifted. After this admission, there was repentance and motivation to not be "that kind of guy."

I have watched great moments of healing occur when a person can accurately speak their confession with connecting emotions and repentance, involving the ways their own sin has altered them, with brothers and sisters who are fellow saints and sinners. I have seen pastors shed loads of guilt and shame they never thought would leave them. "I thought I was taking this to my grave!" I have seen Christian leaders come into a room, shoulders drooping, lifeless expression, staring at the floor, you would think perhaps they were zombies. After confession they leave with fresh air in their lungs, standing tall, faces alight with relief and joy, truly experiencing that Christ took their sin and shame to his grave.

"I DON'T DESERVE THESE WORDS FROM YOU"

Jared was a pastor who came to Marble Retreat because he was caught using pornography. His job was in jeopardy and some of the first responses that he got from people, including his elders, were less than helpful. At first, Jared was more wrapped up in how people were treating him than what he had done. This is normal, but if Jared was going to heal from his sin and shame he needed to focus on himself, not the downfalls of those around him. There were those who judged him, ostracized him, and wanted to be sure a pound of flesh was extracted. But with some nudging he started dealing with himself.

At first Jared spoke in random and generic terms about his pornography use, but as he continued on he dug down into the shame he felt, how he couldn't believe that he would be preparing for a sermon one minute and online the next looking at what should only be seen in the marriage bed. He talked of feeling trapped, hopeless, and dirty. He expressed deep regret for how he had let down those he ministered to, those who believed in him and hired him as pastor, and God. He was heartbroken by how he had defiled God's creation and had used women. The feelings came as Jared spoke. He nearly screamed out the words, "I am such a hypocrite!" The group allowed him to continue on until he was exhausted of words and emotion and sat in his own tormented silence.

To draw him into the community and the community into him, to have them be active participants in Jared's confessional experience, I asked Jared, "What do you think the people in this room think of you after hearing your story? How do they feel about you?"

Jared responded, "They should think, *How could such a man be a pastor?*"

I invited the group to speak. They began pouring out words of encouragement to him, godly words and personal words. Tammy said, "I see the man behind the porn problem and he has a good heart." John added, "Your brokenness over your sin reveals a heart for God and for holiness." And Bellah added, "You are so courageous to be honest. Your sin does not define who you are."

Jared kept his head down, elbows on his knees, his stillness seeming to show he wasn't hearing the words of others. But if you were in that room, you knew he was hearing, more than hearing. He was battling within his soul to either accept the words of the accuser or the words of his family in Christ. His body began to relax. He took a very deep breath and Jared began to cry. He cried different tears now—not of regret and shame, but of relief and healing. Truth and grace had won the battle.

But in the same way that in every superhero movie the villain has to give it one more shot even as they are falling to their death, Jared's shame popped up and he said, "I don't deserve these words from all of you." Someone in the group responded, "No, you don't, Jared, but neither do any of us. That doesn't mean the words are not true. It means they are grace." And they pointed to the cross on the wall, and we all silently worshiped as Jared began quietly saying, "I sing to the Lord a new song, for he has done marvelous things . . ." (Psalm 98:1).

Many in the church would have a negative reaction to how the group responded graciously to Jared. "You are letting him off the hook! He is a pastor and is looking at pornography. Is he even a Christian?"

Unfortunately, this response is what makes the church an unsafe place to disclose your sin. At times the church is like a hospital that treats no one and no one can admit that they are sick. The hospital is full of doctors and nurses and effective treatments, but if a patient says they are feeling sick, they are shamed and told, "We are all fine."

Confession is healing. Forgiveness is healing. Grace is healing. Being reminded that your sins are washed away, taken care of by the cross is healing. Being reminded of who you really are in Christ is healing. Good confession takes us beyond getting off the hook for our sin. It strips away the lie of the accuser and reminds us that our true name is the one our Father and Creator gives us—child of mine, created in my image, fully loved, accepted, and forgiven.

For many Christians confession rarely happens. For the Christian leader, confession almost never happens. This keeps deep healing at arm's length.

CONFESSING OUR SHAME AND BROKENNESS

In a sense Trish felt more shame and regret about not stopping the senior pastor's advances than she did from having a sexual relationship with him. This is appropriate and normal as the victim. His acts shattered her self-confidence. She thought she was a strong, courageous, moral woman with good boundaries. How come she did not speak the truth of what was happening? How could she not say no? How did she let him control her? These questions haunted her.

Trish was so wrapped up in her own shame that she never even mentioned him. It was as if she was the one more deserving of punishment. Ironically, this was a major doorway the senior pastor used to get in—her tendency to blame herself and let others off the hook.

As it usually happens in group intensives, someone (a pastor's wife and quintessential church lady) spoke up and quite intensely said, "I'm really pissed at him! Are you not mad at him for what he did, what he took from you?" Trish sheepishly responded that she had not really thought about it in that way. She supposed she should be angry at him but wasn't.

Somewhere along the way, long before this senior pastor came along, Trish had forfeited her sense of self. She had just never given her body away. She had given everything else, her time, her talents, her comfort . . . Now someone demanded her body and she gave that up as well. She was thinking of him and the church and how everyone would be hurt if she said no, if she "made a scene." She was not thinking of what it was doing to her. In no way am I saying the sexual relationship was Trish's fault. In this situation the senior pastor was holding all the trump cards. What I am saying is that he played her good heart, her willingness to serve and sacrifice, her long history of not valuing herself.

Trish was stuck at this point. She was mired in her own shame, unable to forgive herself or the senior pastor. However, confessing to others revealed the main missing piece. The main missing piece was Trish did not see herself as being important. She needed healing—not just from being a victim of sexual abuse, but from seeing herself as less than and others as more than.

Because she opened up in confession, others were able to minister to her heart and soul. People in the group affirmed her value and worth and beauty. They challenged her to reorient her perspective from "will others be hurt or disappointed if I let them down?" to "what can I offer others if I am whole?" They acknowledged the goodness of her heart in trying to believe the best in others and affirmed the wisdom she was acquiring and added a truckload of their own. They were teaching her how to have the heart of a dove and the shrewdness of a serpent.

Through confession, Trish not only felt absolved of her sin, she experienced an affirmation of her personhood. Not only were the negative labels removed, but also true and good names for her were written on her heart.

REFLECTION QUESTIONS

1. Do you have in place (person, place, time) the ritual of confession? If not, what are the obstacles to doing so? Do you have a safe place where you can share that you are a broken sinner?

2. Do you struggle with fear, doubt, or shame that you are not sharing with someone?
3. Is there a sin currently or in your past from which you do not feel absolution?

9

FALLING APART OR COMING TOGETHER?

KARL WALLENDA, THE HIGH WIRE ARTIST, fell to his death during a show in San Juan, Puerto Rico. In the weeks previous to his death he became worried about falling, even though he had perfected this vocation over decades.

This focus on failure is known as "The Wallenda Factor." Michael McNichols of Fuller Theological Seminary writes in a devotion that

> this focus on failure is a form of forgetting, forgetting about what is most important and what is central in one's work or even in one's life. And also, that sin is at its heart a form of forgetting. Sin emerges through forgetting about God and allowing our eyes to relocate their attention to potential fears and failures, and to attractions that glitter like gold. As Isaiah admonished the people of Israel, "You have forgotten the Lord, your Maker, who stretched out the heavens and laid the foundations of the earth. You fear continually all day long because of the fury of the oppressor, who is

bent on destruction. But where is the fury of the oppressor?" (Isaiah 51:13)[1]

TAKING OUR EYES OFF GOD

McNichols began the devotion with Revelation 2 including verse 4, "Yet I hold this against you: you have forsaken the love you had at first." He draws out how focusing on our sin and failure can take our eyes off God and we can struggle with spiritual laziness and temptation.

There is a paradox in humans when it comes to our sins, brokenness, and weaknesses, which can be heightened, in Christian leaders. The paradox is that while on one hand we are consumed and distracted by our struggles, on the other hand we are working hard to avoid them and pretend they don't exist. The pastor with a pornography problem cannot stop thinking about his problem yet tries his best to ignore it or pretend it isn't there. The reason this paradox exists in Christian leaders is the risk involved in facing personal problems head on and the additional personal shame involved in having struggles in the first place.

One of the downsides of this avoidance is that it leads to disintegration in a person. Disintegration is when there is a breakdown between the different parts of a person. In us humans there is interaction between our thoughts, our feelings, our passions, our souls, our bodies, and our wills. Our thoughts can evaluate and affect our emotions. Our feelings can alert us to a change in will or decision we need to make.

Disintegration negatively impacts the issue being avoided by other parts of us not influencing the problem and breaks down the person in general. Even worse, the disintegration can provide direct fuel for the sin or problem. We were made to live in integrity—where everything aligns including our thoughts, feelings, beliefs, and actions. Disintegration is erosion. It is corrosive to our hearts, minds, and souls.

AVOIDANCE, DISINTEGRATION, AND MORE SIN

Avoidance and disintegration can occur with specific sin or with our general brokenness. Grief is an example of this. Marcy came to Marble Retreat because she was having a mental and emotional breakdown. She was showing signs of paranoia and irrational thinking and volatile emotional shifts. She was proving herself incapable of leading the large women's ministry she had founded. She was irritable with staff and increasingly indecisive.

Marcy had experienced multiple personal losses in the past couple of years including the death of an adult child from a drug overdose, her husband's affair, and a long-term best friend's battle and death from brain cancer.

What was the subtext of Marcy's problem? Marcy had real, legitimate grief, but her personality, the religious culture she was in, the expectations of leading a large ministry, the persona she was expected to display—all ran counter to her experiencing and expressing the "weakness" of grief. To put it simply, Marcy was stuffing it and pushing forward and wrapping her pain in spiritual jargon.

Christian leaders have many reasons to avoid dealing with their pain and problems. There are internal and external pressures and expectations that go with the territory of ministry, in addition to just being pain-avoiding humans.

When a pastor has a sin problem or brokenness such as having experienced childhood abuse, or an area of weakness such as anxiety or depression, the temptation and pressure are great to either avoid or quickly and successfully resolve the problem and turn the victory into a sermon.

This pushing aside of dealing with the defect can be the exact environment the problem needs to flourish. Wrapping pornography use in shame and keeping it a secret. Not sharing thoughts and feelings of depression and anxiety with those close to you. Not displaying feelings of grief after a loss. These reactions feed rather than fix the problem.

And when taken to the extreme one can even push a sin out of their own consciousness. The pressure is so intense for a "successful" pastor to not have a struggle or sin, especially of a sexual nature, that the struggle is denied. This denial gives it life. A life of its own. To counterbalance, the person often becomes super spiritual. The person is acting out or tempted to act out in ways that they don't want to acknowledge and at the same time appear to be growing in their faith and more on fire than ever.

As the division continues, each side becomes more extreme until one is caught or they or their situation blows up in some manner. And as the division or disintegration is occurring everything in one's life is negatively impacted.

HOW DISINTEGRATION PLAYS OUT

To see how the disintegration plays out, let's go back to Marcy. From the overdose of her son to the betrayal of her husband, Marcy had a lot of deep, intense emotions from the losses, embarrassment, and abandonment. She could not or would not directly express these feelings. She also had a lot of theological questions, or more precisely, she had doubts and issues with God. Yet she also did not feel free to directly explore those. And the one person who would have walked with her through all of this, her best friend, was gone.

On the outside, Marcy was trying to portray confidence, victory, and stability. On the inside she was a cauldron full of emotion and confusion. She looked like a dormant volcano, but she was ready to blow. She was cool, impervious-looking rock on the outside and hot, molten lava building pressure on the inside. And the cracks were beginning to show.

THE CRACKS

Mentally. Emotional pain takes a lot of energy and so does critical thinking. All the pain below the surface was using up Marcy's emotional reservoir. Also, the usual mental processes she used including logic, prioritizing, and accurate assessment to make decisions were under attack or doubt. The confidence that she knew what she was doing was ebbing. And not being mentally sharp or emotionally strong she was making some wrong calls on how to handle significant aspects of the ministry. This was increasing her insecurity.

Emotionally. Marcy has always been a passionate person, but not an emotional person. She had always been in control and in many ways used "emotion" as a tool when speaking, teaching, and leading. Now she was experiencing emotions that were controlling her. A small annoyance was invoking rage. A song easily moved her to tears. A memory aroused blind pain. She worked hard to contain these, which somewhat worked except what mostly leaked out was irritability. She was snapping at employees, family members, and baristas.

Spiritually. Renowned for her confident, bold, insightful, and intuitive faith Marcy now could not get a handle on God, her relationship with him, or his Word. She had written a biblically solid book on walking through the valley and now struggled to put one foot in front of the other. She vacillated between thinking she was a fraud to questioning Christianity. She could still say the right things but those closest noticed the difference in how she said them.

Relationally. Being in relationship is about knowing and being known. Marcy didn't have the emotional or mental space for someone else, so she was quick to cut them off if they began sharing their own pain or struggles. On the other hand, she was too exhausted to go into what she was really thinking and feeling. Also, she was scared of losing their respect and trust in her leadership.

Physically. Marcy had always taken pride in her health and felt pressure as a woman leader to appear healthy. Now she wasn't eating healthy, wasn't exercising, and wasn't sleeping well. She did not look well or feel well.

The sum is greater than the parts. Marcy's emotional, intellectual, spiritual, relational, and physical disintegration were adding together to where she was falling apart. Only God's grace and Marcy's grit were holding her together. The first day she came to Marble Retreat she appeared as one with significant mental health issues.

INTEGRATION

Integrating an issue into your life and person and faith often leads to pain but also to healing and wholeness. Integrating means fully facing the problem and allowing all aspects of you to interact with the struggle. It means clearly thinking, feeling, speaking, and wrestling with how one is being impacted by the adversity. It is letting the struggle affect your faith and your faith affect the struggle.

When Peter walked on the water, he focused on the waves and began to sink. He needed to focus on Jesus. Yet focusing on Jesus does not take away your ability to see and feel the waves or have them disturb you; your faith allows you to conquer them.

PATH TO HEALTH

"Marcy, what brings you to Marble Retreat?" I asked.

"I am a mess," she responded. "I can hardly function. I think I am having a mental breakdown."

Marcy was hurting significantly enough to admit there was a problem and she was in a safe place to do it. Over the next few days her story came out. But more importantly her pain came out. Her grief, including anger, anguish, and sorrow, came out in words, tears, and at times groaning. It was heart wracking, even for us observers. It was exhausting. Yet it was integrating her pain and struggle into the rest of her and even into community.

As the days began to pass, her anguish began to lessen. Her countenance began to lighten, she reported a good night's sleep, she began taking care of herself. She began to wrestle with her faith questions. On the last couple of days Marcy joyfully shared she had connected with God and his Word deeply again. She was beginning to see his hand at work again.

Some people need to work through emotional pain before they can fully receive and experience God's presence and believe his truth about their situation. Others need to work things out to a degree with God before they can go deeply into their pain. Meaning many Christian leaders need to know that God is calling and empowering them to face the waves and that doing so is reflective of his way and his Word before they can fully jump out of the boat of their self-protection and fully immerse themselves in the water of their struggle.

Marcy also needed to grapple with the issue beneath the issue. What was it in her that could not accept she had weakness? Why did she work so hard at protecting the image that she had it all together?

She realized it was more for her than for others. She realized this when asked questions to clarify her driving motivations. "What are you fearful of if you are not always confident and have all the answers?" "What are you trying to accomplish by always being the in-control leader? "Are you concerned about what others think of you?" As Marcy sat with questions like these, she realized that she was not a people pleaser or looking for atta-boys. Marcy realized this persona she had created was there for her own security and adequacy. She could draw lines straight back in her history to poverty, growing up on the wrong side of the tracks, having a mother who had men coming and going from their home, and the judgment and shame she experienced at church and at school to see where her fears of not being enough and of failing and being rejected came from. She was not fearful of relational rejection; she was fearful of people rejecting her as a leader. This "strong" image had protected her and had become a sacred cow in her life.

In philosophy there is a concept called GUT—grand unifying theory. It is a theory that explains all the parts. I have found that when it comes to people's brokenness there is often a core belief (lie) that drives everything else. It is like their thesis statement. With some reflection on what fear, shame, or desire drives your dysfunctional behaviors you can often arrive at your statement. Marcy's was "Not being secure (status, job, income, being needed) is the worst thing that can happen and the way to maintain your security is to be strong."

Marcy removed her sacred cow by admitting it was not of God but of this world. She repented of how she had come to idolize her image and her security in herself and not in God. She also began to recognize all the lies she had built up to justify keeping this idol: "I am weak if I show weakness." "God will never use me if I am not strong and confident." "I will lose this ministry if I take it down a notch and not perform like I have."

Dealing with this issue beneath the issue allowed Marcy to accept her weaknesses and begin to trust that God could and would use those however he wanted to. She accepted that most people would not see her as less than . . . but as one of them, and she would not be a worse leader but a better one.

By the time Marcy returned, she was self-assured she was not mentally ill, and her therapists were in agreement. She was clear on the battles she was facing and what support she needed to face them. Her confidence was returning, and she would soon be ready to lead in a new and deeper way with more authenticity and humility. She was integrating the losses and grief into her story instead of pretending they weren't a part of her story or that they were just bit players. She now knew her pain and her struggles and doubts were a big part of her story.

What did Marcy do to move back to health?

Marcy admitted there was a problem, even if she needed some encouragement from others to get to that point.

Marcy sought out help—a safe, confidential, qualified person and place to help her.

Marcy entered her pain and doubts, which began the process of stopping the disintegration.

Marcy recognized the persona she had created and how it had become her sense of security and adequacy. This had kept her from being honest with herself and others about her issues. She dealt with this sacred cow in her life.

Marcy honestly expressed her pain in relationship with others. She needed to grieve and be comforted.

Instead of there being separation between her pain and struggles and her faith, emotions, relationships, and ministry,

Marcy was now integrating these struggles into these areas of her life appropriately. Marcy went from the grief and weakness she had being wrong and her old ways of strength and confidence being right to allowing these to be mixed together to make a bold leader with deep empathy for the pain of others.

Marcy was embracing what God was doing through her story even if she didn't have it all figured out yet.

I heard from Marcy about a year later. She was excited to report that life and ministry were going well. She had worked through a lot of her grief and was enjoying living again. She had begun dating and really liked the relationship. She had started a new ministry for women who are hurting and had written a book and other materials to guide support groups. She believed the new writing was her best work yet with more depth and real-life faith than she had ever been able to write about before. She admitted life and faith were messier now than when she had lived largely under spiritual platitudes, but it was much more full. She said it felt like she was living in freedom.

Christian leaders are at risk for disintegration, and disintegration is one of the reasons ministry leaders blow up. A small spark can light a forest on fire. A "small" issue denied, avoided, ignored can grow into a secret, a shame, an idol, an addiction which can take down a pastor and their ministry.

We all need to deal with our issues.

REFLECTION QUESTIONS

1. Is there a pain or struggle in your life that you avoid dealing with, thinking about, talking about? Are you tired of thinking one thing, feeling another, and doing another?

2. What is the incongruence between this issue and how you do faith and ministry? How do you handle that incongruence?

3. What would living with integrity (where thoughts, feelings, and actions are in line) look like in your life and ministry?

4. If you look at the dysfunction or brokenness that at times drives you, can you summarize it in a sentence? What is the fundamental lie behind it?

5. Marcy had lies and fears that drove her resistance to not incorporate her grief into her faith and leadership. "People will not respect me." "It will reveal weakness." What are the fears that keep you from dealing with _____?

6. Do you have a person with whom you can work out and talk through the contradictions you are experiencing in your life?

10

DEPRESSION AND SUICIDE

I am fearful of getting well. I think people's
expectations of me will only increase.

PASTOR STRUGGLING WITH DEPRESSION
AND MINISTRY EXHAUSTION

My brain is broken and I cannot take it anymore.

FINAL POST OF TEXAN METEOROLOGIST
BEFORE TAKING HER OWN LIFE

T HE DAY HAD ARRIVED. Pastor Aaron had thought on and off about the idea of suicide for nearly two years now. He often thought about ending his own life when he believed he couldn't think past the next step. When times were tough he envisioned getting over that next mountain. In the last six months his musings were real. He determined the day and the time and how. He was not nervous; he was sad. Actually, he had a sense of relief.

He couldn't tell you how he had gotten to this point. It seemed inconceivable to him. There were factors he was aware of that played into his despair; his personal, private pain seemed beyond those. But his pain was real and he couldn't handle it anymore. He was convinced that everyone would be better with him gone and that this was the only option before him.

He had prepared everything. He had planned for his family to be out of town. He'd written the letters. He'd planned his method, one he felt would be foolproof. He stopped and decided to pray one more time. The act of praying seemed strange, distant. He'd prayed thousands of prayers for healing and deliverance over the years and some time ago had given up on praying regularly, if at all. He did still lead public prayers as part of his role as pastor. Out of compulsion or desperation he began offering up his final prayer.

His phone buzzed. He glanced at it. A text from his buddy Finn. Finn and he had been in seminary together and were both pastors now. They touched base from time to time. While not regularly in close contact, Aaron considered Finn his best friend. "How ya doin'?" the text read. Aaron's first thought was to ignore it and continue with the plan. Phone buzzed again. Text read, "I am on the road and have some time to talk. Can I give you a call?"

While Aaron believed nothing was going to change what he was about to do, he was prompted to reply, "Sure." His phone then rang. It was Finn. Though he was a thousand miles away, he was now with Aaron in his darkened thoughts. At first Finn asked innocent "catch up with your life" questions but quickly realized something was wrong.

"Are you okay, Aaron?"

Aaron thought about a last, neutral response to get Finn off the phone. But then he decided to open up a bit about what was going on. He shared some more. And before the end of the

124

conversation Finn had Aaron promising that he wouldn't hurt himself before Finn was able to get there.

The tide would turn for Aaron that day. He didn't realize it, but it was his first step on the road to recovery, one that was not just avoiding suicide for another day.

HOW CAN THIS HAPPEN?

It breaks my heart that there even needs to be a chapter on this topic, but it is too real to leave out. If you are in the Christian world, especially the Christian leadership world, you either know of a pastor or other Christian leader who has taken their life such as Jarrid Wilson or Darrin Patrick or you have seen the stories. It has become too common.

It's not my purpose to write about the diagnosis or detection of suicide. There are plenty of online sites and a lot of written, audio, and video resources out there to help people determine if they're struggling enough to reach out and get the help of others.[1] I am trying to give a picture and help explain a few of the most obvious whys of this tragedy for Christian leadership for those of us looking on, for the church in general, and for the ones who can't speak for themselves.

Why do Christian leaders take their own lives? When anyone ends their life at their own hands, there are always more questions than answers. Yet when it comes to a Christian leader, the "why" seems to stand out even more intensely.

How could they do this? Did they not have hope and faith in Christ? Could they not have leaned on their brothers and sisters in Christ? Did they not know that God was with them in whatever they were facing? Did they not realize that in Christ they had forgiveness from sins and healing from fear and shame available to them?

In our work with Christian leaders we have come to know a few of the reasons some wrestle so deeply with the temptation to take their own life. Do these insights provide all of the answers? No. There is not an answer that covers everything. The self-ending of life by Christian leaders is not supposed to happen and no answer we try to give can explain it or make it right. But I'd like all of us to get some understanding and compassion and direction on how we as a church can help stop another one of her shepherds from taking their own life.

SOME OF THE WHY

Pastors die by suicide because they are human. Being a pastor doesn't somehow guard you from the struggles of life. There's no silver bullet for this situation, either. In 2018 over forty-eight thousand people in the United States died by suicide. Pastors do this for many of the same reasons as others in making what is a fatal choice.

One of the reasons people in general turn to suicide are the overwhelming feelings of pain they feel daily. Many pastors experience this. They are overwhelmed by the amount and type of problems and people they need to face. They patiently hear about other people's struggles, grief, losses, and sin. Pastors are called upon to come into hospitals and emergency room situations. They are there when there has been domestic abuse or child abuse. They're confidants of those who hurt and those who have hurt others. It is a lot of pain to carry.

And then the pressure. The pressure to bring hope, healing, and answers to all kinds of pressure-filled situations: how conflict can be handled between two families, how an answer can be given on the spot to a family facing a life-changing circumstance like the death of a loved one. You name it, pastors have a lot of pressure and expectations on them. As I quoted a pastor above, "I am fearful of getting well. I think people's expectations of me will only increase." In his mind, he lived under unbearable pressure. Being sick was a way to have people back off a bit. The thought of taking your life is another way to get out from under this pressure.

Many Christian leaders have shared how they have turned to alcohol to help deal with the daily pressure they are experiencing.

"I drink a half-dozen beers an evening to help me come down."

"I can't get the day out of my head until I have three-quarters of a bottle of wine."

While portraying itself as temporary relief, alcohol is a depressant and brings on the feelings of the depression one is running from. And it opens the door to addiction.

Addiction is the perfect storm situation for a pastor to begin wrestling with the idea of suicide. For anyone addiction brings feelings of hopelessness, helplessness, and shame. "What is wrong with me, why can't I stop relying on drinking? Taking pills to get up each day?" For the Christian leader, the despair around addiction is intensified knowing that if they confess and get help it will mean the end of their job. The feelings of failure can be unbearable; they are supposed to be stronger, full of faith.

When a pastor is caught in addiction—alcohol, pornography, or sex (work and food addiction are still currently acceptable in the ministry)—they are caught between the addiction that they cannot control and the loss of their calling and livelihood, and suicide can become a way out of being trapped.

WHY PASTORS DON'T JUST LEAVE THE PRESSURE

If a pastor finds their role so pressure filled, then why don't they just leave and go work at Home Depot or something?

Having sat with many wrestling with just that question of leaving ministry, I know there are reasons why that is so difficult. One reason has to do with their belief in "calling." Many in ministry believe that they were called specifically by God to do the ministry they've chosen. To leave and do something else feels as if they are betraying God. Reinforcing staying in the ministry even when they are unwell is the belief that if they are called then God will provide. They have hope that God is going to come through and change things at any time. So while on one hand they are desperate to get out, there's almost nothing that will stop them from hanging in there.

The pastor also does not want to let down those they are serving. Pastors find themselves encouraging others to believe when times get tough. Pastors place that example in front of church members. And pastors sincerely want to continue to be the pastor of those they have come to love and serve. For many pastors, leaving their church feels like a divorce, even if the marriage is killing them.

Most pastors cannot tell anyone how deeply they are struggling. Part of the reason is what Matthew West captured in his recent song "The Truth Be Told," which talks about not being okay but everyone saying we are okay. We just do not get that honest and messy in church and especially not the pastor. And once again the pastor believes he is letting people down by not being stronger or healthier. He has taught his sheep how their faith can help them with the trials of life, and yet he thinks if he's struggling he is a hypocrite.

Some Christian leaders who die by suicide have a mental health issue going on that is not being treated at all or inadequately. While their faith has an effect on their mental health struggles, it is not always the complete answer because the mental health problem is not completely a faith problem. While it is still not fully accepted by every Christian group, many have come to understand struggles such as depression, anxiety, and bipolar disorder have partly or largely a physiological cause. Many Christian leaders we have worked with have benefited greatly from intervening in their mental health struggle from a faith perspective, getting counseling, and by seeing a psychiatrist who prescribes medication to address the physical problem.

Many Christian leaders are not comfortable accepting that they have a mental health problem. And they are frightened to go public and address it. Some still frame their struggle as a lack of faith. They feverishly try to grow their faith while their mental health issue rages on. The meteorologist quoted above took her life because she lived being trapped in the pain and hopelessness of having a "broken brain" and having been a victim of abuse. Pastors can be there as well.

I've written that many Christian leaders have been the victims of abuse in their childhood and have never dealt with how that affected them. Abuse, especially severe abuse, deeply disturbs a person in their affect, relationships, and general sense of whether the world is safe or not. If abuse is not treated specifically, the world is definitely a painful place to be, and it is that much easier to consider leaving it.

Perhaps the most life-stealing condition one can experience is deep shame. We are ashamed yet we don't want to just leave. And yet shame causes us to want to withdraw and hide. Shame convinces us there is something wrong with us beyond our sinful nature. It says we *are* bad.

One of the dynamics pushing pastors over the edge toward taking their own life is their own belief and then condemnation that they should not be struggling. "I have faith, I know Jesus, I am forgiven, I have my family, I have a congregation to which I belong, therefore I have no right to feel the way I am feeling."

PART TWO — PROBLEMS IN MINISTRY

While others may raise the question of how a pastor could kill themselves when they know the Lord, the pastor himself has most likely wrestled deeply with this question and come out with a shame-based answer. "What in the hell is wrong with me that I don't take peace, pleasure, confidence from my faith and what God has given me?" They shame themselves for not feeling better and doing better, which only serves to deepen their despair.

HOW CAN WE HELP?

A friend of mine posted a Henry Cloud quote on Facebook: "A wasted day is one where we only thought about how someone else should change." When I read it, I thought, *Dang, as a counselor all I do every day is think about how other people can change, so guess I am wasting every day.*

While I may think about how others can change, I have learned as a therapist that I can never control how other people react, decide, or what they do. What we can do is try our best to help as well as we can and most importantly, love as best as we can. We cannot stop hurting folks from taking their lives, but we can learn to better love those who are at risk and hope that in doing so, fewer will make that awful choice.

In a sense Matthew West's song is a plea to the church, "Can we just get honest?" He says the pews would be full if we did. He is probably right. One of the first and most important ways to care well for ministry leaders at risk is to give them permission and the safety to be honest.

I worked with a ministry leader who had the dual diagnosis of depression and anxiety. His sharing deeply about his struggles was a great relief. Bringing his demons into relationship broke through the shame he felt. And broke through the loneliness and isolation he was experiencing in this battle. While openly sharing about your mental health may seem obvious and a natural step to the general public, it is not common for the Christian leader. For the leader, there is great power in relieving this burden.

On the first morning of counseling we introduce ourselves to those who have come and say something to the effect of, "This is a safe place. We are here for you, not for anyone else." Often there are audible sighs in the room and sometimes tears just at realizing they are no longer alone.

Pastors need emotional, physical, relational, educational, financial, and other helps that are some of the sources of their problems. We have worked with Christian leaders who have struggled with addiction and began their journey to recovery here and then returned and joined AA, Celebrate Recovery, or other support groups. And pastors who were burned out and depressed from working outside their gifting and passion who went on to take classes and spend more ministry time doing things that gave them life. And pastors who were overweight and began weight loss classes and started walking every day. And pastors who began a support group at their own church to help others with the exact issue they were seeking healing in. Not only did these pastors get well, God used the journey to transform them and their church.

There is help!

To provide the right support the church needs to continue to grow in its understanding and teaching of who we are as humans. A better grasp regarding how we are made up of body, mind, soul, spirit, and heart and how these all interplay can be crucial in our reactions to those who are hurting and what we provide. All parts of us can be broken, and one broken part can affect another. Scripture does not only focus on the spiritual, and we as a church could do better in addressing all parts of being human.

Understanding that we are humans and that we are broken is part of compassion for those who struggle with mental illness. Our founders, Louis and Melissa McBurney, who opened Marble Retreat in 1974, purposefully named it Marble Retreat instead of Marble Counseling Center knowing that many pastors might lose their jobs if they shared they were going to counseling. They could say instead that they were going to a retreat in Colorado.

Today, many of our Christian leader clients come on the advice of those around them and with their support. I have seen folks in denominations who ten years ago would have argued that bipolar disorder does not exist coming to realize that it is real and has a biological component. There is hope that the church is becoming a safer and more helpful place for those who struggle, including its leaders.

THERE CAN NEVER BE A BIG ENOUGH SAFETY NET

I've talked about safe places for sharing. But there is a next step. Leaders who have struggled and have been helped need to share their stories. I understand their fear and apprehension in doing so, and everyone must make this decision for themselves based on their own situation. Yet if more Christian leaders shared how they have battled depression, anxiety, suicidal thoughts, or worked through their abuse, this sharing would help normalize problems and give hope to those who are struggling. Many pastors I have worked with struggle with shame because they are not as strong, confident, as full of faith as pastor so-and-so, not knowing that pastor so-and-so has battled depression and is on medicine.

In the church we are family. We are to love one another and help one another. If we can accept others, including our leaders, in their brokenness and commit to being there for them, to listen to them, to walk with them in their journey through trials, they will feel safe and be on the road to healing.

Many pastors have lost their view of how they are valuable to God and to others. It's the old "when I perform, when I do what I am called to do, that's when I am valuable." They struggle to embrace first and foremost that they are a child to be loved. Those around the Christian leader can reinforce that they are valuable because of what they do for us and for the church. And we, the church body, can help by letting our Christian leaders know we understand they are human and need support and are valuable even if they are not performing well.

We can make a great difference in our struggling pastors' lives when they know they are not alone in their pain. When a pastor sees their brother or sister in Christ and can say, "They still love me, though they know my struggles," it can make all the difference.

INTO THE DARKNESS

Pastor Solomon struggled with sexual addiction. Like many men with this issue it started in his teen years. He was exposed to his dad's pornography at a young age and his dad's sexual gratification philosophy: you get as much as you can when you can. Solomon had found the Lord, or more accurately, the Lord found him in college. He grew in his faith and ultimately believed he was called into ministry.

Solomon got married, had kids, and was the pastor of a church in Idaho. He had seasons of sobriety from pornography and sexually acting out, but it was always lurking in the background, his little secret, until it wasn't lurking invisibly anymore.

Solomon was caught going to a strip joint. His elders wanted to give him a redemptive chance, so while they removed him of his preaching and teaching duties for a season, they kept him on staff. There were boundaries and expectations for Solomon including therapy and a support group. Solomon was relieved momentarily at the grace and support he experienced. Yet he felt fear about what was going to happen in his marriage and ministry, he felt shame at the fact that people now knew his dirtiest secret, and he was experiencing a lot of self-condemnation for what he had done now that the ramifications were hitting his wife, kids, and church.

Addiction does not just leave. The shame of being exposed and the pressure to get well led him to act out again. He was driving home from the massage parlor. He was playing out the conversation with his wife and then the elders in his head. How could he have done this? He just abused their grace and wasted the opportunity they had given him. A semi truck was coming his way. Solomon swerved into its path, causing a head-on collision. Solomon was gone.

A LETTER TO THE ONE CONSIDERING SUICIDE

If you are reading this and suicide is something you are contemplating, the first thing I want to say is that I am sorry. I am sorry that life has become unbearable. I am sorry for how you have been hurt and disappointed by the fallenness of the church, others, and yourself. I am sorry for the pain you feel as you cry out, "This is not the way it is supposed to be."

You are right it is not supposed to be this way. Those of us in the kingdom should have more experiences of love, acceptance, peace, and wholeness. It is so difficult when most of what we seem to experience is pain, heartbreak, and disappointment. I am sorry that the dark cloud of depression has settled on you and you cannot find your way out. Or the terror of gripping anxiety has you wanting to get out of your own skin. Maybe the cloud and the terrors are both there. I know there seems to be no way out, and like the psalmist in lament or Job, your longing for death is understandable.

But please don't do it. Don't take your own life.

There is hope. I know you don't feel it now—that you cannot see it and have not for a long time. I know it seems like you are trapped in the misery of the pain you are feeling and there is no way out. And I know it feels like I am throwing a cup of water at a forest fire and hoping it will help. But there is hope.

Someday it will get better.

How do I know this? Because I have sat with many who have either attempted suicide or were contemplating it and were so glad that they didn't go forward with a plan or that their attempt didn't work. They couldn't see the change coming at the time but later experienced it.

I think of a pastor who was in a toxic ministry and his wife was cheating on him. He just wanted to die and could see no other way out than taking his life. Today he is in a new ministry and his marriage is restored. He is so glad he held in there.

And I think of when I was in hospice ministry sitting at the bedside of those in their last days, some of whom had been suicidal in their lives, but they had battled through life and could now see the purpose in why and had the satisfaction they had made it until God called them home. There is hope that things will change at some point.

There is help. I don't know what you have tried and perhaps it feels like you have tried everything. And I know that it is hard to even think about trying something else. It is hard to find the hope and energy to give it another chance. It is hard to once again set yourself up for disappointment. But there is something out there, someone out there who can help.

I worked with a pastor so deeply stuck in his anxiety and depression that he could see no other way for relief. He had been on his knees, been to psychiatrists, taken a break from ministry and nothing was helping. He just felt more shame and despondency from all the attempts to stop the bleeding. With the support and encouragement of family, friends, and counselor he tried a new medication, changed some job responsibilities, and more diligently invested in his relational and recreational life. The cloud began to lift. Looking back he could not believe what had changed in six months.

You are loved more than you know. When trapped in your depression and anxiety you cannot feel the good things of life, including the love of those around you. But it is not true that you are not loved. You are deeply loved, by God, by your family, and most likely by many in the church. I know many who struggle with suicide believe that because of their emotional battle they are not being a good spouse, parent, friend, or pastor and that the people they care about deserve better. But these people love you! They want you. Having sat with those who lost a loved one to suicide, I can affirm that they just wished their loved one could have heard, seen, and felt how much they love them and now how much they miss them. You are loved more than you know or currently feel. Someday you will be able to see that love and feel it again.

No one knows or understands what it is like for you. How every day is battle to just survive. How going to bed at night is not relief but a painful reminder of how dark everything is as you lie there stuck in your own personal nightmare. Every day you choose life is a victory. Every day you choose to not take your life you are winning the battle against despair and hopelessness and are one day closer to a change and relief.

And while this can sound like theological jargon, there is one who gets it: Jesus. He felt the full burden of the sin and brokenness of this world. He despaired of life itself. He entered the darkest of the dark in the grave. He does get it and he is with you in your tomb. There is resurrection coming. Please hang in there. Some day you will be so thankful that you did.

Please reach out and tell someone.

REFLECTION QUESTIONS

1. Are you depressed? If you are concerned that you might be, you can take this inventory: https://counsellingresource .com/quizzes/depression-testing/goldberg-depression/

2. If you are struggling with depression, have you had earlier episodes in your life, or do you believe it is situational to your current circumstances?

3. Are you open to considering medication if needed? What are the obstacles you would need to work through to consider medication?

4. Have you told someone? Who is the first person you could tell that you are struggling?

5. Is your church open to discussing and understanding mental health issues? If not, what is the first step you could take in helping the church grow in this area?

PART THREE

DEFUSED

Known and Loved

11

IDENTITY AND
ADEQUACY IN CHRIST

ALLIE'S MINDSET IN LIFE IS "not too bad is good enough." She never has been the driven or perfectionistic type and feels alone when her ministry counterparts' motto is "good enough isn't good enough." Was she gifted? Yes. Was she called? Yes. Did she have an effect on those in the kingdom? Yes. Her heart was pastoral and her love, compassion, and kindness naturally flowed in her pastoral care role. Her passion and concern for others was evident in her weekly blog.

Allie could never quite get comfortable with who she was. She believed that she should be more. She thought she was missing out on all God had for her by not being more assertive and more of a risk taker—by expanding her kingdom. This feeling of falling short had gnawed at her for a long time but recently had hit a crescendo.

Ironically, what pushed Allie over the edge was finally taking the plunge and committing to a couple of big projects in her life. She was now doing what she believed she should have been doing—pushing herself. She signed a contract to write a blog for a major Christian online magazine. She began promoting herself as a speaker for women's conferences.

Instead of the elation she was hoping to experience by stepping out in faith, Allie was overwhelmed and fearful. It was hard for her to see herself as the image she was creating. And it was hard for her to produce under pressure. Her worst struggle was she didn't like who she was becoming—irritable with people, focused on projects instead of relationships, spending more time in front of a computer than praying by sick people's bedsides.

It is an interesting and beautiful phenomenon when God uses the exact experience that is torturing us to instigate healing and bring us back to him. Allie was at a women's conference and was slated to speak. It was an hour before she was to walk on stage. She was in her room on the verge of a panic attack. While she desired to perfect her talk, her anxiety was making concentration hard to come by.

She decided to go out and listen to the worship. As she was moved into God's presence and out of her fear, she relaxed. As sometimes happens in Spirit-led worship, one song hit Allie hard, in a good way. It spoke of God's loving kindness and un-conditional acceptance. Allie closed her eyes and saw herself at the podium and the thousands of expectant faces before her. Her anxiety began to tick up. Then in her vision she saw Jesus was standing beside her on the stage. Then she looked back at the crowd and every face had become his face and they were all smiling back at her. She got the point, loud and clear.

In that moment, Allie began the journey of realizing it does not matter the opportunity or challenge that lies ahead. What matters is who you are doing it for and who you are doing it with. It is not letting your personal insecurity or other's expectations define how you feel about yourself; it is letting who you are in Christ define you.

IDENTITY AND ADEQUACY IN CHRIST

Most pastors start out being well grounded in who they are in Christ, meaning their relationship with Christ is the lens through which they see themselves and is their motivation for serving. They know Christ, give their lives to him, believe they are called into full-time ministry, and feel blessed to be able to serve him and the kingdom. They love getting to know him more and his Word deeper. They desire to share the good news with as many as possible and to love those who are already in the family.

SOUL QUESTIONS

Several questions are built into the DNA of our souls, into the genetics of our personhood. One of the first developmental accomplishments of our seven-month-old son Easton was learning to smile. Anthropologists would probably argue this is a survival mechanism to help babies be valued and cared for or part of the mirroring they do to learn from us. I believe it reflects their design by God to be relational, to love and be loved, to connect.

Three questions we all carry around are, Who am I? Am I loved and valued? And am I adequate and acceptable? We go through life trying to figure out who we are. After we have come to believe in God the Creator and us the created, the question has to do with how I am wired, or you could say designed. What is unique about me? What makes me tick? What is my purpose and place in the kingdom? One of the main reasons I continued in school and pursued different degrees was in trying to answer this question. It was a process of seeking and trying until something fit.

And hopefully we grow in self-acceptance. I went from believing I am too introverted, not smart enough, don't have a good enough memory, and my negative interpretation of other weaknesses and traits to seeing who God had made me to be and how he was growing me.

And when I learned who I really was, got comfortable in my own skin, then I could experience being truly loved and valued. When we are unsure of who we are or not liking who we are, we are often working hard to be something or someone else. Just being ourselves allows others to love the real us. At one point in my adult life, my grandmother said to me and about me, "Mike is Mike." I took it as a compliment, but with my grandmother you didn't always know!

Ultimately I came to know who I was, accept that I am loved, valued, and acceptable because I trusted in God, his creating of me, his providence and that through the redemptive work of Christ we have the answers to these heart questions. He defines us. In him we find our true identity. We are loved and valued. We are accepted. Like sanctification, it is also a process I am continuing to grow into.

However, for multiple reasons, the chief being that we are imperfect sinners wanting to play God's role, we look for more. There has got to be more is the lie we are sold.

Performance, control, production, knowledge, accumulation, accomplishment, adrenaline—you name it. We have come up with lots of ways to add to Christ and his redeeming and defining work on the cross.

OUR TRUE IDENTITY

The river that runs through Marble, Colorado, is called the Crystal River. It was named such because it is so clear. When fly-fishing the Crystal you can often see the trout. It is fun to walk upstream behind them, watching them before casting the fly in front of their mouths. The only time the Crystal is not clear is during runoff, when the snow is melting quickly or there is a big rain and then mud gets in the water, making it hard to see.

Scripture is crystal clear on our true identity, from creation to fall to redemption through Christ. Yet this world, the evil one, or our own broken selves can muddy the waters of Scripture, but if we look, we can see the truth clearly.

What does Scripture tell us about who we truly are? "Yet to all who did receive him, to those who believed in his name, he gave the right to become children of God" (John 1:12). We are his children. This is a fundamental and foundational truth of our identity. And in case we have any misconceptions about God's motivation in having us as children like it was some cosmic accident or because someone had to do it, we are told, "He predestined us for adoption to sonship through Jesus Christ, in accordance with his pleasure and will" (Ephesians 1:5). God created us and redeemed us because he wanted to—really wanted to. We are wanted. "See what great love the Father has lavished on us, that we should be called children of God! " (1 John 3:1).

What are we like as God's children? "So God created mankind in his own image, in the image of God he created them; male and female he created them" (Genesis 1:27). We are made in his image. Unbelievable. Yes, through Adam we fell, but our fallenness is not a reflection of who we really are; our likeness to him reveals who we really are.

Our adoption or redemption back to our Father gives us an intimate relationship with him. "But whoever is united with the Lord is one with him in spirit" (1 Corinthians 6:17).

And we belong to a family with the surname Christ which defines who we are and how we live. "Now you are the body of Christ and each one of you is a part of it" (1 Corinthians 12:27).

145

"But you are a chosen people, a royal priesthood, a holy nation, God's special possession, that you may declare the praises of him who called you out of darkness into his wonderful light" (1 Peter 2:9).

These few verses show us we are children of God, we are made in God's image, we are the body of Christ, we are one with Christ, we are a chosen people, a royal priesthood, a holy nation, God's special possession. And what is God's heart behind giving us this identity? His love. His pleasure. His will.

If we have drifted off, how do we come back to letting Christ be our identity and adequacy?

FINDING OURSELVES

One path back to Christ is to rid ourselves of whatever else has been providing our identity.

Pastor Trevor was wrestling with this question. Trevor had believed he was called into the ministry from a young age. He is a quiet guy, introverted. He is intelligent but does not wear his smarts so all can see. He is humble, sacrificial, and hardworking. Trevor has pastored in three different churches. In the first two he had been an associate and in this last church he was the lead and only pastor on staff. It was a small church in rural Missouri. He and his family like it there.

Trevor had been there for four years when one night at the weekly elders meeting all the elders turned their chairs to focus on him. He felt the immediate change of climate in the room. The lead elder began to speak. Trevor does not remember much after that except a few phrases like "this is not working out," "we need someone with a different gift set," and "three months' severance." He was a deer in the headlights.

Trevor was devastated. The most painful phone call thus far in his life was calling his wife as he drove home to tell her what happened. He knew the church was not growing but otherwise thought it was going well. His family was tired of moving. His wife and kids had made friends here, and they really appreciated the supportive school system.

Trevor and his family moved out of the parsonage but decided to stay in the area for now. Trevor was working as a delivery truck driver. He was tempted to be mad at the elders, but at the end of the day it was more natural for him to blame himself. How come he wasn't more dynamic? Why couldn't he grow the church?

When he came to Marble, in addition to fixing his family relationships that were now strained, the main issue he desired to work on was his faith in God. He was deeply troubled by wondering if having Christ was really enough for him at the end of the day.

Pastor Trevor was lost. Even in ministry Trevor had questioned his purpose as he never appeared to be successful. When he was let go, the bit of self-worth he had was gone. He deeply grieved the losses. He floundered like Peter in the waves. He was sinking. He cried out. Jesus reached out and grabbed his hand.

A person does not need to lose their ministry in order to return to and live out of their relationship with Christ. Human nature is such though, that often it does take an earthquake to split the foundation we have built our house upon to force us to reconsider or even notice it has been sand all along.

Here are some steps one can take to move back toward identification in Christ.

First, we need to realize the extent to which we have let other gods define us and give us our worth. "Define yourself radically as one beloved by God. This is the true self. Every other identity is illusion," wrote Brennan Manning.[1] In a sense Manning is saying that everything we add to "one beloved of God" is fluff at best and potentially misleading ourselves to base our identity on lies.

Often, for the Christian leader, the "other identity" is our work. Tim Keller explains one of the dangers in this, "If our identity is in our work, rather than Christ, success will go to our heads, and failure will go to our hearts."[2]

The most disastrous effect that our pressure-filled ministry has on us Christian leaders is that we no longer wholeheartedly pursue knowing God, but rather we wholeheartedly pursue how to be good at ministry.

Second, we need to repent and grieve and let go of this "god." Repentance is conviction and the desire to change. Grief is the process of detaching emotional connection from something. For many there is a lot of emotional connection to their inappropriate relationship with ministry or their approach to life and ministry. I have worked with many pastors who are burned out or having high anxiety, including panic attacks, and a big reason was the pressure of their perfectionism: "I have to do this right every time!" While God was their God, perfectionism was their religion and dictated how they did things more than any other value. As one pastor said, "Letting go of perfectionism is like saying goodbye to an old friend." This old friend was a constant guide and was good at being a guide, actually perfect, but led him the wrong way.

When an influence other than our relationship with Christ becomes the driving force in ministry we need to repent and grieve and change.

Third, we need to feel our need, our lostness, and our dependency again and correspondingly experience Christ again and again and again. "Blessed are the poor in spirit. . . . Blessed are those who mourn" (Matthew 5:3-4). When the earthly supports are taken away or denied that have been propping up our egos, we have the opportunity to experience our own emptiness again, and Christ's fullness. Ironically often when one becomes good at ministry, one does not see or feel their need for Christ.

Experiences can get us into trouble and experiences can help get us out. Bad experiences in life feed our shame, fear, and sin. To rewrite our hearts, souls, and minds we need experience, experience of God's truth, grace, and love. God's truth is the program. Experience is the download. To experience one needs to get real and vulnerable with God and community.

The point I am making is this: we know theologically that through Christ we have identity and adequacy. To drive home these truths, we need to experience intimacy with him.

Pain can lead us to deeper places that can open us up to experiencing God again. Pastor Trevor went from worrying about his situation and how to fix it, to questioning where he was at with God. Driving in the truck he began to reflect on who was he if he wasn't a pastor? Would God ever use him again? Was being in Christ truly enough, and what does that even mean in his situation? Was his love for Christ his main motivation in ministry? Was Christ's love for him what he valued most?

During his time with us Trevor unpacked carrying the shame of being fired and the pain of letting down his family. He had a lot of fear that he would not find another job in ministry. As he dug deeper into his pain and guilt and fear, he became more desperate for grace and forgiveness and for an affirmation from God that he was loved, heard, and that God was there for him.

God did not disappoint. In many ways God revealed his care for Trevor in the days ahead. From the Word coming alive again and specific verses jumping off the page and being exactly what he needed, to another group member spontaneously picking up a guitar to lead the group in worship and beginning with Trevor's favorite praise song, to experiencing the weight of guilt and shame being lifted from his heart by crying out and taking these burdens to the cross. He experienced God's tender and powerful presence sitting outside in a starlit night in the background of the Rocky Mountains. And the icing on the cake was that Trevor, who had never been to the mountains, wanted to see a bear. His second to last day with us, returning from a hike, he saw a bear in the serviceberry bushes near the trail.

These experiences were much more than feel-good moments. They spoke directly to Trevor's heart and encouraged his faith. He experienced that Christ was present with him and in loving, gentle ways. He discovered that a "bruised reed he will not break" (Isaiah 42:3). It was like a husband and wife who have drifted apart due to the responsibilities of life and then one day look at each other and realize that they are still deeply in love but had neglected their relationship. Jesus had affirmed his love for Trevor. And Trevor was savoring it.

DEEPER HEALING

Pastor Trevor was hard on himself. While there has been some change in this, overall society, including church society, does not value the introvert as they do the extrovert. This only helped feed his deep personal insecurity. While his sermons were biblical, well thought out, and practical, he constantly rode himself about his self-perception of having an Eeyore delivery, even making self-deprecating remarks from the pulpit. "If you are having trouble sleeping you may want to get copies of today's message." "I am preaching through Lamentations, finally a book that lines up with my disposition." He also saw all the other ways he fell short in ministry.

While Trevor and our group were digging around in this shame spot in his heart here at Marble, the Lord kept bringing the Scripture of Psalm 147:10-11 to his attention. "His pleasure is not in the strength of the horse, nor his delight in the legs of the warrior; the Lord delights in those who fear him, who put their hope in his unfailing love." Trevor began meditating on these verses. He could not get away from them. Why was God bringing it to his attention? What did it mean?

Being an introvert, Trevor did not share any of this with the group or his wife. Moving as the Spirit does, another group member came in one morning and shared with the group, but especially Trevor that they had been led to share a Scripture with Trevor. Of course, it was Psalm 147:10-11. Not only did this have the immediate result of driving home to Trevor that Christ was pursuing him with this passage, but it also opened up the opportunity for the group to help Trevor understand what this might mean specifically for him.

Trevor had experienced healing for the immediate wound that brought him to Marble—his being let go. But he also experienced healing in a lifelong wound—his lie of inadequacy. His identity and adequacy in Christ were reestablished, or should we say, he was reminded of these in an intimate, real, and powerful way.

When one opens up a painful place, a place of shame, a place where a lie resides, and experiences God and his truth in that moment and place and then carries this truth and experience forward, it moves from head to heart. It brings healing for the past, present, and the future. This moves your experience of your identity back to where it belongs, to seeing yourself as God sees you.

BEAUTY REVEALED

When a Christian leader fully embraces their freedom in Christ, they become who they were truly created to be. No longer driven by unanswered soul questions, they can rest in who God says they are and the specific calling he has for them. Out of our identity should come our work and not vice versa. When we get these in the right order we will find joy, peace, and confidence in "the good works God prepared for us in advance to do" (Ephesians 2:10 paraphrased).

It is a beautiful sight to behold when one becomes who they were created to be and casts off the sin and shame of this world by seeing themselves and their ministry through the eyes of Christ.

REFLECTION QUESTIONS

1. Are you experiencing your fundamental identity as a child of God, made in God's image and redeemed through Christ? If not, what is the road block?

2. What helps you to experience your identity and design? Worship? Community? Creating?

3. Do you use shame to motivate yourself? "I should . . ."

4. Does living in freedom and acceptance seem too good to be true? If you are trapped in shame, what is the shame? Can you name it?

5. Do you find yourself thinking that you deserve to fail, be rejected, not be liked, not be respected? Or are you fearful of whether people will like you or believe in you? What truth from God or your own experience contradicts these fears?

6. Imagine yourself walking in freedom. What concern or fear does that raise? That you will become proud? That you will need to be more assertive? That you will take more risks?

KNOWING OURSELVES
AND BEING KNOWN

G OD KNOWS HIMSELF. He is the great Three in One. He knows who he is intimately.

Do we? Do we really know who we are, in ourselves? Or do we place so much distance in between who we think we are and who we really are that we don't know the difference?

If we do not know ourselves, how then can we be known? Ask Christian leaders their theology—they know. Ask them their ministry approach—they know. Ask them their mission and vision statement—they know. Ask them who they are outside of the role of pastor—sometimes they don't know. It is true that the Enneagram and other such inventories have helped many know more about themselves.

A pastor may know themselves well except in their area of brokenness. Brokenness, meaning in ways we are damaged or wounded, or our sin and shortcomings. Correspondingly others may know pastors well, except for their areas of brokenness.

This was the case with Norman.

NORMAN

Norman came to Marble Retreat for ministry burnout. Normal enough issue. What is never "normal" is the journey one took to get to burnout, meaning while there are common paths to burnout, the reasons you are on the path vary by person.

Norman was the senior preaching pastor of a church of 250 people. He had one associate and an office manager. Norman had recently hit a wall and was not able to function in his responsibilities.

Norman had been at this church for eight years. His predecessor had been there for thirty. His predecessor was the founder and a very loved man. But he was not good with money. The church was in enormous debt, and Norman happened to be good with finances. Norman was the preacher and he did the hospital visits and funerals. He led the elders and he was involved on the local school board. The associate took care of young adults and youth.

Norman's denominational background was less than friendly to emotional weakness and emotions in general. This had been fine with Norman, a man more prone to wear logical arguments on his sleeve than his heart.

Norman was struggling to focus on work, to make decisions, and he was experiencing anxiety. He believed he could not share what he was going through with others. He tried for a long time to continue powering through, hoping he would eventually snap out of it. He didn't. His internal emotional distress increased, and he regularly found himself sitting at his desk frozen, staring, unable to move forward on anything. He was a mess of anxious energy on the inside but paralyzed on the outside.

It all came to a head at an elders meeting. They were digging into the financials and were asking Pastor Norman about the refinancing of the church's debt he was supposed to do. He had not done it. It had been too much for him to concentrate on and decide. As the elders innocently asked questions, Norman lost it. He blew a gasket. The elders sat there staring in disbelief during and after Norman's rant, which covered everything from the founding pastor's ineptness to his own sense of being over-whelmed to the lack of appreciation from the congregation for what he does, to how boneless chicken wings are inappropriately named because they are not boneless.

Norman came to Marble Retreat to work on his burnout. We looked at the reasons for his burnout—lack of boundaries, taking on himself the responsibility to fix everything, not asking for help, not confiding in anyone of his struggles, including his wife, not emoting and staying in his head, and not deeply connecting with others. The question remained—what had caused these dynamics in Norman? Why were they so strong in him, more than just tendencies?

In a session Norman tentatively offered a possible cause, though he was doubtful. He told us an older boy in his family had sexually abused him as a boy, over quite a long period. But he immediately followed up this admission with "But I am over it, I forgave him, and I don't think it has really impacted me or impacts me today."

"Why don't you think it impacts you, Norman?" I asked.

"Because I never think about it. Never crosses my mind and wouldn't have except you guys have been digging around in our pasts."

One of the sad and perplexing experiences of counseling Christian leaders is how many of them have been sexually abused as children. Lifeway Research found from interviewing one thousand pastors in 2018 that 20 percent of them had been the victims of sexual or domestic violence.[1] The perplexing part is how many of them have never dealt with it in any purposeful way and how many of them have never told anyone about it, including their spouses. They thought the best way to deal with it was to work hard to move on as if it is having no effect. In doing this they do not realize the impact of being sexually abused has on issues like attachment, boundaries, power and control, intimacy, and self-worth and shame. Those issues are alive and kicking today even if the memory of the abuse has been pushed far away.[2]

If you have abuse in your background you may overreact to authority figures in your life. This overreaction can all be internal, but you know you are being deeply affected. You may swing to extremes on boundaries, from struggling to say no to setting very hard boundaries. You will most likely deal with shame and fear when it comes to your boundaries, your needs, and your feelings. This can come out in not sharing these or in being so uncomfortable sharing these that you overstate or even demand. And you also may swing in your attachment to others from staying aloof to feeling overly attached and affected by those you minister with and to.

Norman could have sworn that there was no effect today from those events long ago. Yet he was living out many of the reactions of a sexual abuse survivor. And part of his pushing it aside is that he did not want to be defined or seen as a sexual abuse survivor. While the sexual abuse he experienced did not need to define him, it was part of his story, a significant part.

Often in group therapy one person is aware of how the abuse they experienced is affecting them, or they have decided to deal with it head-on for the first time in their lives. As they begin sharing their abuse story it is interesting to see how others in the room are reacting. There is usually deep compassion, but there is also a growing discomfort among those who have never dealt with their own abuse. This intimate sharing eventually encourages those who have abuse in their story to deal with it. It is one of the blessings of being with openly broken people—it reveals to you your own brokenness and gives you the courage to face it.

KNOWING YOURSELF IN YOUR BROKENNESS

Many Christian leaders do not know their own brokenness very well.

Pastors can use their faith to hold their wounds and sins at arm's length. I have forgiven. I have repented. I am in the Promised Land and am no longer a slave in Egypt. Yet as someone once said, you may have left Egypt and are in the Promised Land, but you still have some sand in your sandals.

Norman and all Christian leaders need to have their brokenness addressed. They need to recognize the wounds, sin, losses, and other life blows that have damaged them, causing them to limp around emotionally, spiritually, or relationally. It is so helpful to them to connect the dots from their past injuries or fallenness or weakness to their struggles today.

Often there is a wrong identification of the causes of today's problems. "I am just not good at relationships" when really there is an attachment wound. "I struggle with empathy" when a person has never experienced nurturance from parents and does not know how to enter another's pain. "I don't have enough faith to take big risks in ministry" not knowing how growing up in a household of fear and control is playing into how they do life. Often these wrongfully assumed causes are sources of shame for the leader.

Spending time wrestling and reflecting within safe and healthy community can often help a person to discover the real causes of their struggles. Not only in sharing your story can others help you connect dots in ways that you are not seeing, they can also reflect back what they do see and experience in you that perhaps you are unaware of. While this can happen naturally within a community or especially a therapeutic group one can also purposefully enter into this experience with others using a tool like the Johari Window. It is an exercise in which you and others who know you choose from a list of adjectives to describe yourself.

It is a relief when one realizes the connection between the main cause and their current struggles. We have worked with many Christian leaders who had a true mental health issue such as major depressive disorder, bipolar, attachment disorder, or PTSD. When hearing their diagnosis for the first time you would expect shock and fear, but more often it is relief. "I have been beating myself up about this for years and made it into a character issue. I shamed myself for not having more energy when it was depression." "I should have more control over my emotions," when they had bipolar disorder. "Knowing there are other reasons for my behavior gives me hope."

To even get to the point of connecting the dots a pastor needs to open up to someone, have someone look inside their life. And usually to get well it takes ongoing interaction with community. Many pastors we work with return to their homes and begin attending Celebrate Recovery[3] or some other form of support group realizing their need to get well in relationship. Even if they must do this in another town to feel safe.

When Norman opened up about his abuse with the group, he experienced compassion and understanding that he had never known before. With some input he was connecting more dots than he ever had. He had wondered why he reacted the way he did in certain situations and seemed so powerless to stop it. Once his wife was over the shock of this revelation, as a couple they began putting the puzzle pieces together regarding their dance around intimacy in their life. Norman was able to truly begin healing from a shame he had carried his whole life. And he finally knew the right target to be aiming at in improving his life—his abuse.

KNOWING AND BEING KNOWN

If I had to pick one important key to healing, then I would choose this—being deeply known by another. And to be known by others we must know ourselves, and we will only understand ourselves fully and deeply through relationship with others. Knowing and being known build on each other. Why is God in trinitarian form? In constant togetherness? Why don't God, Jesus, and the Holy Spirit just hang out once and awhile instead? There must be something very good about being known, about being together. God made us to be in relationship. God created the church body as a place to find healing—a place to be known and ministered to in a way specific to who we are.

When someone knows someone, they know their struggles, their personality, and what they need to hear or have done for them. Have we not all experienced this with best friends? It is probably why they are our best friend—they know us well and how to love us. They know when we need someone to listen, to hear something funny, to get a kick in the butt, or to just be offered chocolate.

For many of the pastors we work with, others know them through their role. For many of the missionaries we work with they do not have someone or some people with which to share deeply of their stories, their pain, and their successes. When they begin to share their autobiography and experience being heard and known it is powerful. Regularly after someone has shared, they will look at us and the other members of the group and gush, "Thank you, thank you so much for listening." It is like a long-lost and forgotten part of their heart was just touched and brought back to life.

One of the dynamics in healing the bottom of the iceberg problems in our lives is this one: the experience of being known. Hard to explain yet so crucial to healing. The experience of intimacy is healing in itself. And if we need someone to accurately help us, how can they do it well if they do not know us?

Yes, there are times when God speaks to us through his Word or Spirit and it was the exact thing we needed to hear. It pierced through. And there are times when a preacher or other person says something to a crowd and it is the exact thing we needed to hear as prompted by the Spirit.

But often God uses someone we have let inside, someone who is holding our pain responsibly, someone who has taken the time and effort to get to know us, to speak exactly what we need for healing. Their words are like a scalpel in surgery—specific and focused and penetrating and effective.

It is hard to capture what happens spontaneously when the Spirit blows where the Spirit wants to blow. Often the most powerful healing thing that happens for someone is when another person has a Spirit-driven response in the moment. Frequently this happens when you know someone's heart and compassionately react with a word of truth, a hug, a tear, or silence.

A ministry leader and his wife were here for affair recovery. He was the adulterer. His wife, Emma, decided to forgive him and stay with the marriage. The second-most excruciating wound after his betrayal that she experienced during this season was from several Christian women who were shaming her for her choice to remain his wife.

"You should leave him."

"You are being a doormat."

"You should at least kick him out for a while."

I am guessing these women were fearful that Emma was being taken advantage of. They didn't realize what their criticism was doing to her as she tried to make and then stick with the most difficult and painful decision of her life, when she needed the support and encouragement of her sisters in Christ.

One session after Emma had visited this wound, I was moved to say, "Emma, you are a strong woman. It is not out of weakness, fear, or insecurity that you made this decision to forgive and stay with your husband. It is out of faith, love, and a commitment you have to your vows. Hold your head high, feel no shame in what you are doing. God is pleased with you. You are taking the road less traveled, the Christian way."

Emma does not remember the other ten thousand words I said during her time at Marble. She remembers these. And these happened because I knew her heart and her wound and was moved by the Spirit to say something from my heart.

Folks come to us counselors with deep struggles in their hearts, lives, relationships, and ministries. On the first day they download what brings them to Marble and some of their story. On day two they are ready for us to fix them. There are a lot of general truths we could share with them about their challenges, but we don't yet know them. We don't know what they struggle with the most about their situation and why. We don't know their personality. We don't know enough of their history to tell us why their experiences are being filtered the way that they are. In short, we don't know what their heart needs for healing and how God might use us in that healing.

When either my wife or I have said something to someone that was truly powerful, it was not from some preconceived counseling intervention or general truth. It was our hearts connecting with theirs and the Spirit prompting us to speak.

For this to happen, I need to know their story. I needed to know the places of hurt and confusion. I need to be in relationship with the person. I also need to know God's heart, God's truth about the person's place of need. The person needs to be honest and vulnerable with their story, and they need to be open to hearing from someone else.

"What are the significant losses in your life?"

"How did that change you?"

"What drives you?"

"When are you at peace?"

"Have you experienced being deeply loved? Tell us about it."

"When did Christ become real in your life? How did it happen?"

"How were you called into ministry? How would you define your calling?"

"What regrets in life do you have?"

"Can you put words to those tears?"

"What did you hear about yourself in that interaction?"

"What is your biggest fear about yourself, your ministry?"

"Tell us about your mother and your father." (Yes, standard counselor question, but we gotta ask it.)

These are some of the questions we ask and many more to learn what is going on in a person's heart, mind, and soul.

One of the most important pieces of the puzzle in healing the deepest places of hurt in our hearts and souls cannot be broken down into steps. It happens in relationship. It happens in reaction to someone else. It happens in spontaneous connection. It happens when we know and are known.

And the most important part about being known is that it is instrumental in the most powerful cure of the issues beneath the issues—being loved and loving.

REFLECTION QUESTIONS

1. Do you think that you are known, really known by someone?
2. God knows us. How can you experience his knowing?
3. Is there an area of your life, a trauma or experience, where you struggle to know how it is a part of you?
4. Do you need to see a therapist or someone similar to understand a part of you?
5. Is there an area of your life that you avoid thinking about or telling anyone about?
6. "Blessed are those who mourn, for they will be comforted" (Matthew 5:4). Is there some healing you are missing because you are not bringing a piece of yourself into relationship?

BEING LOVED
AND LOVING

Love builds up.

1 CORINTHIANS 8:1

For to build up means to draw forth something from the ground up,
but spirituallly love is the ground of everything. *No man can bestow*
the ground of love in another man's heart; nevertheless, love is the
ground, and one can build up only from the ground up; therefore
one can build up only by presupposing love. Take love away—
then there is no one who builds up and no one who is built up.

SØREN KIERKEGAARD

It is by loving and not by being loved that one
can come nearest to the soul of another.

GEORGE MacDONALD

I define love thus: The will to extend one's self for the purpose
of nurturing one's own or another's spiritual growth.

M. SCOTT PECK, *THE ROAD LESS TRAVELED*

A PASTOR IS A CHILD OF GOD. A pastor is made in God's image. A pastor is first a child to be loved, not a tool to be used.

Just being loved. We are uncomfortable with this. Can't we earn it? Shouldn't we have to earn it? Are we not more lovable when we act better, do better, smell better?

There are many ironies in the life of a Christian leader, some of them cruel. One of those cruel ironies is that while many Christian leaders are admired, and you could say liked, many are not deeply loved. They have an arms-length relationship with those around them.

One of the questions we sometimes ask those we work with is, "When was the last time you experienced being loved?" Typically, the response we get from a pastor is when they have received positive attention for a job well done. "When we finished the building project and the church held a celebration," "When I preached at a beloved member's funeral," or "When we celebrated twenty-five years of ministry at this church/missions" are the kind of answers that come. While there is nothing wrong with these, there is something missing.

Our next questions ferret out the missing part, "When was the last time you experienced being loved in your brokenness? When you really messed up? When you blew the sermon at the building dedication? When you forgot a VIP's name? When you got caught using pornography?" Many cannot come up with an example of being loved in brokenness. This unfortunately reveals a very harsh and ironic truth—many pastors are not loved for who they are, but for what they do.

The irony is that by themselves and others, pastors are expected to love others very well. We worked with a pastor of a large church that specializes in being a safe, graceful place with multiple ministries for sexual brokenness including support groups, materials, and twelve-step groups. He laid the foundation for the congregation to care for those who are broken. Then he fell. Got caught using pornography. They fired him and asked him to leave. "Clean out your desk within three days. Don't contact anyone at the church or we will take the severance package away."

I mentioned in the last chapter how important it is to be known in the healing process. If one is not known, how can one be ministered to? If one has not brought their sin, shame, pain, and wounds into the light of relationship, how can they be healed? The most important opportunity being known opens up is the opportunity to be loved. At the end of the day, the only healing balm for our hearts is loving and being loved. To be loved well, others must know you. For our deepest wounds to be healed we must be loved in that broken place. At the end of the day we cannot fix people and people cannot fix us, but we can love them, and that is even better.

Jesus does not love us despite our brokenness; he loves us right where it hurts. Look at how he loved the woman caught in adultery right in the midst of her shame and condemnation, how he loved Zacchaeus in his ostracism from those around him, how he loved Peter in his denials, how he loved Saul in his persecution of the church, how he loved the rich young ruler in his struggle with love of possessions. Jesus, instead of throwing some vague general healing at someone, walks right into his or her most wounded place and offers love and healing.

SAM

Sam is a stud. Intelligent, athletic, good-looking, and a dynamic speaker. Everything he put his hand to turned to gold. He was the rising star in his denomination and already a popular speaker at pastor conferences. Sam is envied by others. He has it made. Yet Sam was miserable. He was disillusioned with ministry and his growing resentment was creeping into his faith.

Early on, Sam was able to maintain a level of humility even with all his positive attributes and much admiration from others. Now he was growing in arrogance. He was beginning to cut corners. He had always believed that the ends don't justify the means. But with increased pressure and opportunities combined with his growing arrogance, Sam started taking chances and he was doing this in many areas. A little plagiarism, less tight boundaries with women, and taking a little more pay for himself than was in his contract are some of the ways he was playing fast and loose.

Sam was gifted and attractive. The Christian world often parallels the secular world when it comes to folks with these traits in that their behaviors revealing deeper problems are overlooked. Sam was a racehorse and was winning. No one around him wanted him to stop or do it differently because he was leading the ministry into growth and new opportunities.

Sam continued on this path toward destruction. He had learned the equation for success in ministry, but unfortunately that is exactly all it was becoming, an equation. He was bored with his ministry show. He was tired of playing people, knowing if he said something catchy or got "passionate" in his message that the applause would come. It had become a game to him.

This playing the system went back a long way for Sam. Unfortunately, a potential dark side of being attractive and having a charismatic personality is knowing how to use it and at the exact same time feeling used by others for these traits. Sam had mixed feelings about himself, and having an insecure, angry, and critical man as a father who repeatedly told Sam he was a fake and was just getting by on his good looks only intensified the wound. At a deep level Sam believed him.

The growing disparity for Sam between who he felt he needed to be for ministry and the loneliness, frustration, and doubt he was experiencing on the inside were tearing him apart. He was starting to choke on his own hypocrisy. In short, Sam now hated himself.

When Sam first began opening up about his disillusionment with ministry and self-denigration in group counseling, you could see others didn't really believe him or at least struggled to accept the depth of his agony. They saw the outside of Sam and like many, thought he had it made. What does he have to feel shame about? It can be hard for us to accept another's struggle when it appears to stand in stark contrast to what we see and have concluded. When a model talks of her poor body image, when an accomplished singer shares of his insecurity about how he sounds, or when Sam spoke of his self-hatred. Our group was astounded by Sam's comments. How could Sam with all he had going feel this way about himself? His unbelievable confession got in the way of our empathy and understanding, as it would for others.

But as Sam dug deeper into his story and as his pain became more palpable and his self-condemnation so strong it was like watching someone publicly undressing to reveal the body they were ashamed of, others began to lean into Sam—the broken Sam.

As others did get to know the broken Sam and express empathy, concern, and encouragement, an interesting thing began to happen. Sam began to feel not so bad about himself. As Sam brought the deepest part of his shame into the light of relationship and he experienced love and acceptance instead of the condemnation he was experiencing from himself and expecting from others, his shame began to heal.

Shame is a funny thing though. While Sam was embracing the acceptance he was experiencing from others, he was also uncomfortable with it. As if to test the acceptance he one day blurted out, "But don't you think that I am a fake? Can't you see that?" Leonard, another pastor in the group, warmly and firmly said to Sam, "Sam, you have been anything but a fake during this time. You have been honest, vulnerable, and authentic. Because of your courage to be real about your struggles I have been encouraged to also be real about mine. So no, I do not think you are a fake. I think the real Sam is the one we have been experiencing and if others experienced this Sam they would respect him like I do."

Sam's biggest lie was that he was a fake and that if people knew this he would be rejected. This fed the pressure to keep faking it, to give people what he thought they wanted. Yet when Sam was known and loved in this area of shame, he experienced healing. He was now free to be who God had truly made him to be.

Being loved. This is what it is all about. More than just the driving force behind movies, books, and music, it is the driving force behind the universe, and the cross. It is why God sent his Son. It is why Christ came, because he loved us. As Søren Kierkegaard said,

> For to build up means to draw forth something from the ground up, but *spiritually love is the ground of everything.* No man can bestow the ground of love in another man's heart; nevertheless, love is the ground, and one can build up only from the ground up; therefore one can build up only by presupposing love. *Take love away—then there is no one who builds up and no one who is built up.*[1]

Love builds up. When we are face-to-face with the ruins of our own brokenness, we are seeking to be built up. For beauty to come from ashes, for dancing to come from mourning. It is love that builds us up—from the ground up. And one incredible aspect of love is that it not only raises the one being built but also the builder.

BROTHERS IN ARMS

Leonard was in the same counseling intensive as Sam. Leonard was thirty-five years Sam's senior. He has served in ministry for over forty years. Leonard was a quiet, unassuming man. He had served humbly in several small parishes during his call. He was now nearing retirement and did not know his next place to serve in the kingdom. The lack of a next assignment and no one pursuing him to serve somewhere had hit Leonard with a sense of uselessness. And he would say it out loud, "I guess I am not useful to anyone anymore." He would try and wrap his pain in humor, so he would smile while he made statements like "Guess all an old preacher can do is be a Walmart greeter" or "About the only one waiting for me to show up is the mortuary." But he was fooling no one; the despair oozed out of him.

Leonard was also fooling no one about his perceived uselessness. He quickly became important to the group. He became a father figure to the others. When Andrea, a young missionary, was tearful about the violence she had seen on the field, Leonard asked if he could pray for her and he lifted up the sweetest, most encouraging prayer she had ever heard. He ended the prayer with a word of blessing, encouragement, and protection on her. When a young pastor lamented his falling into pornography use and his fear that God would never use him again, Leonard shared some of his own sin as a young man and how God had forgiven him and went on to use him in ministry in spite of his sin and even redeemed the sin by having Leonard help others who struggled.

Sam treasured Leonard. Sam watched Leonard. In Leonard Sam saw the father he wished he could have. But more than that, Sam saw the opposite in Leonard of all he hated about himself. Sam saw himself as a fake, as one who hides behind his looks and personality. In Leonard he saw sincerity, humility, true wisdom, and Christlikeness. Leonard was becoming Sam's hero, one he longed to learn from and imitate.

Sometimes feelings from another relationship, often from a historical and important relationship like in your family of origin, can be transferred to a current relationship. This extra dynamic can be detrimental, but it can also be very powerful and healing.

When we become Christian we become part of a new family. I am sure God has many reasons for this. One reason I see is that if we are doing family as Jesus asked us to by loving one another (John 13:34), we can find and receive the relational nurturing we may not have received as children. In the body, God can provide a father, a mother, a sister, or brother. And Sam needed a father.

On the second-to-last day of the intensive, someone asked Leonard to tell them about some of his favorite ministry experiences. It was an expression of care for him, valuing his story and his service. And the younger pastors in the room were gathering up the wisdom to be gleaned from his years of experience.

Leonard talked of leading young rebellious men to the Lord who went on to become pastors and missionaries themselves. He shared of his time at a small rural church in Arkansas where he was often paid in rice and corn rather than cash. He talked of baptisms, weddings, and funerals, including doing one with an

Elvis Presley impersonator on a Harley Davidson. Leonard was smiling, glowing, as he reflected on how God had used him.

As quick and painful as a sucker punch to the stomach, a thought hit him. He was done. There would be no more baptisms, weddings, and church services where he was the pastor. In a moment Leonard went from recalling the heights of his kingdom experiences to the grief of thinking that it was all over. We saw him stop talking midsentence, his face turned pale, and his head fell into his hands.

Initially this sudden change silenced the group. Then Andrea, the missionary, quietly asked Leonard, "Can you tell us what is wrong?" Slowly Leonard, more to honor the request than out of his own desire, shared, "I love ministry. I love preaching, teaching, and being a part of people's lives. But now it is over. This current calling is over and there will not be another one. No one wants me. No one needs me. I just feel useless . . ."

"Stop it! Just stop it!" Sam nearly yelled as he popped out of his seat and took steps toward Leonard. Leonard looked up, not knowing whether to be mad, scared, or hurt. But Sam had his attention. Sam went on: "That is a lie, Leonard! You are not useless. Look what you have done for this group. You have encouraged us, prayed for us, shared your wisdom with us. You have done more to help me as a pastor in these last seven days than anyone ever has. You are everything I hope to be someday. The church needs you. We need you. I need you. I love you, Leonard."

Sam himself was caught off guard by his own words and the passion behind them. He began to feel awkward and embarrassed, thinking he had crossed a line. He began to slowly back up toward his seat, intending to sit down and disappear. As Sam was about to sit down, Leonard said, "Wait!" and slowly got up out of his seat and walked over to Sam.

172

For a moment they stood face-to-face. Finally Leonard said, "Thank you, Sam." He reached out his arms and Sam stepped into his embrace. Leonard had one more thing to say to Sam as he held him: "Sam, I am proud of you. I am proud of you, son."

LOVE AND BE LOVED

To love another is to invest in their spiritual growth. It is to help them in being who God designed them to be, who they are in Christ. A person's sin, shame, fear, and brokenness warp their own sense of identity, their worth, their true design. When we can love them in and through their brokenness, and bring grace, truth, and love to those places, we help them to be all God planned for them to be. God designed and intended love to heal the giver and the receiver.

Sam needed a father figure. He needed someone who believed in him, who invested in him, who saw him for who he truly was and could be. Leonard lovingly provided that. Leonard desired to still be used and useful. He desired to be a part of people's lives. He did not want his love, wisdom, and experience to go to waste. In loving Sam he found what he needed, and in Sam's loving him he received value and affirmation. When Sam and Leonard arrived seven days earlier their heads were hanging, hearts were hurting, and hopelessness reigned. When they walked out the door after sharing, knowing each other, being loved, and loving, their heads were high, hearts were full, and the world was again full of hope and confidence.

Christian leaders typically do not need more information, another intervention, another program to go on their shelves. They need to love and be loved deeply. Not only does love defuse the issues beneath the issues, love makes beauty from ashes and dancing from mourning. We become more like ourselves. We become more like him.

Jesus knows our big need—we were sinners ostracized from God. And he knows our specific needs, where each one of us requires his love and power for change and redemption. He meets these needs. He provides the cure for the issues beneath the issues.

REFLECTION QUESTIONS

1. How do you define love? Has ministry redefined it for you? How do you see Christ loving others, or how do you see him asking to be loved?
2. When you think of people who love you, what names come to mind? How do you experience their love?
3. When was the last time you felt God's love? What helps you experience his love?
4. Do you make relationships that are marked by love a priority?
5. Do you have a safe place to be loved in your brokenness?
6. Do you have opportunity to deeply love others?

EPILOGUE

MANY PASTORS QUIETLY AND HUMBLY serve out their years in ministry. No scandals and no fanfare mark their service. They faithfully teach the Word and love those God has entrusted to them. Others blow up and leave ministry. And still others participate in God's redemptive work particularly in and through their brokenness and more fully become the people and pastors God intended them to be.

Pastor Lionel is one of those pastors. Lionel had all the high-risk factors for burning out and exploding in ministry. He grew up in a very abusive home, which became many homes, as he was removed from the abuse in his biological home and placed in the foster system at a young age. This childhood left scars including deep insecurity and fear. He had ADHD and addictive tendencies, and for twelve years—from his teens into his twenties—he was actively addicted to alcohol and drugs. It was during this time that Jesus found him, and Lionel gave his life to Christ and then committed to the ministry.

Lionel was well aware of his struggles, and he embraced a lifelong journey of growth and healing. Step groups, accountability, marriage counseling, reading books on his issues, you name it and he did it in the goal to be well. While he still "walked with a limp" he walked and even ran at times.

The depth of his struggles informed his ministry, his messages. The freedom and confidence from the victories God gave him infused hope into his heart which bled on to others. His limp kept him humble when God blessed his ministry and expanded his territory.

Lionel was navigating his risk factors as well as possible. Here are some of the characteristics I saw present in Lionel that not only mitigated his brokenness but turned it into a strength. First, he was deeply in love with Christ and he deeply received Christ's love. Christ's Spirit permeated him and transformed any potential shame or guilt he might have wrestled with. Second, he learned how to really connect with people and have intimate relationships. And out of this flowed a comfort and valuing of asking for help when he needed it. He came to Marble Retreat because he had experienced a "hostile takeover" of a ministry he had started. He knew his heart could get caught up in bitterness, grief, and doubt, so he asked for help to stay well and put out lit fuses.

Lionel saw God's work in and through his struggles. Instead of his history and battles being perceived as negatives in his life as a pastor, he saw how God's strength flowed through his weaknesses. His "go big or go home" attitude, which is a part of the addictive mindset, allowed him to take big risks and start new ministries, his ADHD gave him advantages in multitasking, and his journey informed a practical and profound faith.

Pastor Lionel fully realized he was a weak vessel containing influence and power. He knew if he did not stay dependent on God, aware of and dealing with the state of his own heart, and involving others in his walk, that could blow up. He also confidently knew if he did these things, the dangers could be defused, and God would be glorified in his life and ministry.

These things are true for Lionel. They have been true for me and for countless others. And they can be true for you.

ACKNOWLEDGMENTS

I WOULD LIKE TO THANK the incredible team at InterVarsity Press led by Dr. Al Hsu. Your guidance through this process was invaluable.

I would also like to thank John Sloan who helped with editing the original manuscript. Your passion for this project and love of literature and storytelling helped mold this book and kept me believing that this was worth accomplishing.

I want to thank those who have led the way before us in the area of caring for Christian leaders, especially Louis and Melissa McBurney, the founders of Marble Retreat, and Steve and Patti Cappa, our predecessors at Marble Retreat. You all showed us how to deeply care for the folks who come here by deeply caring for us.

I also would like to thank our staff at Marble Retreat including my wife, Kari, Bob and Lisa Rue, and Cheryl Yarrow. We have such an incredible team that all work together to create such a caring environment for those who are hurting. I also want to thank our board of directors. Your support of us and belief in us has helped us face many challenges and continue this great ministry. You are like family.

I want to thank all the pastors, missionaries, and other Christian leaders who we have met with and gotten to know. You are inspiring, you are salt of the earth, you are people of the Word. It is our privilege to serve you as you carry the kingdom forth in this broken world.

Finally, I want to thank my parents, William and Ida MacKenzie, who taught me about what is most important in life and to appreciate a good story. And my brother, Robert MacKenzie, who ventured into ministry first and has shown me it is okay to face challenges and change in life.

NOTES

INTRODUCTION: THE POWERS AND THE DANGERS IN THE LIVES OF PASTORS

[1]Wendell Berry, *What Are People For?* (Berkeley, CA: CounterPoint, 1990), 9.

1 HOW ONE PASTOR BLEW UP

[1]Barna Group, The State of Pastors: How Today's Faith Leaders Are Navigating Life and Leadership in an Age of Complexity (Ventura, CA: Barna, 2017), 11.

2 GOING IT ALONE

[1]Wendell Berry, *The Art of the Common Place: The Agrarian Essays* (Berkeley, CA: CounterPoint, 2002), 99.

[2]Michael MacKenzie, "Curriculum for Pastor Care Specialists Addressing Significant Pastor Issues," (DMin project, Lincoln Christian Seminary, 2009), 103.

[3]Lisa Cannon Green, "Former Pastors Report Lack of Support Led to Abandoning Pastorate," *LifeWay Research*, January 12, 2016, www .lifewayresearch.com/2016/01/12/former-pastors-report-lack-of -support-led-to-abandoning-pastorate.

[4]Bob Burns, Tasha Chapman, and Donald Guthrie, *Resilient Ministry* (Downers Grove, IL: InterVarsity Press, 2013), 346.

[5]Henri Nouwen, *Turn My Mourning into Dancing* (Nashville, TN. Thomas Nelson, 2001), 89.

[6]S. M. Johnson, *Emotionally Focused Couple Therapy with Trauma Survivors: Strengthening Attachment Bonds* (New York: The Guilford Press, 2005), 3.

3 SHOT BY THE SILVER BULLET

[1]Personal communication, 2/5/2021, used with permission.
[2]Personal communication, 2/25/2021, used with permission.

4 THE FUSE IS LIT

[1]If you desire to take the life stress test, you can find it here: www.stress .org/holmes-rahe-stress-inventory.
[2]Thank you to Troy Harding, US Army for your help in clarifying this metaphor.
[3]Christopher Adams, Holly Hough, Rae Jean Proeschold-Bell, Jia Yao, and Melanie Kolkin, "Clergy Burnout: A Comparison Study with Other Helping Professions," *Pastoral Psychology* 66, no. 2 (April 2017): 147-75.
[4]Lisa Cannon Green, "Despite Stresses, Few Pastors Give Up on Ministry," *Lifeway Research* September, 1, 2015, http://lifewayresearch.com /2015/09/01/despite-stresses-few-pastors-give-up-on-ministry/.
[5]Green, "Despite Stresses."
[6]Joseph W. Ciarrocchi and Robert J. Wicks, *Psychotherapy with Priests, Protestant Clergy, and Catholic Religious: A Practical Guide* (Madison, Connecticut: Psychosocial Press, 2000).
[7]Bob Burns, Tasha Chapman, and Donald Guthrie, *Resilient Ministry* (Downers Grove, IL: InterVarsity Press, 2013), 128.
[8]Burns, Chapman, and Guthrie, *Resilient Ministry*, 511.
[9]Lisa Cannon Green, "Former Pastors Report Lack of Support Led to Abandoning Pastorate," *LifeWay Research*, January 12, 2016, www .lifewayresearch.com/2016/01/12/former-pastors-report-lack-of-support -led-to-abandoning-pastorate.
[10]Charles Stone, "What's Wrong with People Pleasing?" *Christianity Today*, Winter 2014, accessed January 15, 2021, www.christianitytoday.com /pastors/2014/winter/whats-wrong-with-people-pleasing.html.
[11]H. B. London Jr. and Neil B. Wiseman, *Pastors at Greater Risk* (Grand Rapids, MI: Baker Books, 2003), 172.

5 MEGAPASTORS: THE FALLOUT FROM A MEGATON BOMB

[1]Bob Russell, *After 50 Years of Ministry: 7 Things I'd Do Differently and 7 Things I'd Do the Same*, (Chicago: Moody, 2016).
[2]Jeremy David Johnson, "The Connection Between Lead Pastors' Enneagram Personality Type and Congregation Size" (EdD dissertation, Southeastern University, 2019), 37, https://firescholars.seu.edu/coe/37.

[3]This quote is often attributed to Arthur Schopenhauer but its origins are actually unknown.

9 FALLING APART OR COMING TOGETHER?

[1]Michael McNichols, "Rung #18: On Spiritual Laziness & Stagnation," The 2020 Lent Project, Biola University Center for Christianity, Culture, and the Arts, March 21, 2020, http://ccca.biola.edu/lent/2020/#day-mar-21.

10 DEPRESSION AND SUICIDE

[1]Here is one place to start for help: https://suicidepreventionlifeline .org/.

11 IDENTITY AND ADEQUACY IN CHRIST

[1]Brennan Manning, *Abba's Child* (Colorado Springs, Co: NavPress, 2015), 49.
[2]Keller, Tim. 2015. "Facebook Post." Facebook, September 14, 2015, www .facebook.com/TimKellerNYC/posts/if-our-identity-is-in-our-work -rather-than-christ-success-will-go-to-our-heads-a/1017411044965448/.

12 KNOWING OURSELVES AND BEING KNOWN

[1]Bob Smietana, "Pastors More Likely to Address Domestic Violence, Still Lack Training," *Lifeway Research,* September 18, 2018, https://lifeway research.com/2018/09/18/pastors-more-likely-to-address-domestic -violence-still-lack-training/.
[2]If this is your story, you may want to read *Understanding Sexual Abuse: A Guide for Ministry Leaders and Survivors* by Tim Hein (Downers Grove, IL: InterVarsity Press, 2018).
[3]To find a Celebrate Recovery group near you, visit www.celebraterecovery .com/crgroups.

13 BEING LOVED AND LOVING

[1]Søren Kierkegaard, *Works of Love* (New York: HarperCollins, 2009), 212.

ABOUT THE AUTHOR

M ICHAEL MACKENZIE was born and raised in Prince Edward Island, Canada. He came to the United States in 1993 to pursue an education in Christian counseling and since then has served in various ministry and counseling roles. Since 2002 Michael and his wife, Kari, have specialized in caring for Christian leaders.

ABOUT
MARBLE RETREAT

MARBLE **R**ETREAT WAS FOUNDED in 1974 by Louis and Melissa McBurney, who were called by God to provide a safe and beautiful place for pastors and missionaries in crisis to receive counseling. It is our goal to bring healing to hurting pastors, couples, and families through our intensive crisis counseling program. If you or your spouse is in the midst of a crisis or trial that is threatening to disrupt or blow up your ministry, please reach out to us today. We are here to help you through this difficult time.

Our mission is to help bring healing, hope, and restoration to those in vocational Christian ministry and the church at large in our retreat center in the mountains of Marble, Colorado.

Marble Retreat runs year round and has helped over five thousand pastors, missionaries, and lay pastors. No matter the trial that you are facing today, we are here to help you through it. Our program directors Mike and Kari MacKenzie have helped others just like you restore their lives, families, and ministries:

- dealing with depression and burnout, compassion fatigue, trauma on the mission field

- marital conflict (restoration following an affair, communication problems, etc.)

- vocational issues (forced termination, midlife crisis, thinking of leaving ministry, etc.)
- sexual problems, including pornography use

No matter what situation that you are struggling with, Marble Retreat can help you recover and thrive again in your ministry.

A proud member of the American Association of Christian Counselors.

marbleretreat.org
ministrycare@MarbleRetreat.org
facebook.com/marbleretreat